A SINGLE MAN

based on the book by
Christopher Isherwood

adapted by Simon Reade

‖SAMUEL FRENCH‖

Copyright © 2022 by Christopher Isherwood and Simon Reade
All Rights Reserved
Photography: Michael Wharley
Artwork Design: Rebecca Pitt

A SINGLE MAN is fully protected under the copyright laws of the British Commonwealth, including Canada, the United States of America, and all other countries of the Copyright Union. All rights, including professional and amateur stage productions, recitation, lecturing, public reading, motion picture, radio broadcasting, television, online/digital production, and the rights of translation into foreign languages are strictly reserved.

ISBN 978-0-573-13373-2

concordtheatricals.co.uk
concordtheatricals.com

FOR AMATEUR PRODUCTION ENQUIRIES

UNITED KINGDOM AND WORLD
EXCLUDING NORTH AMERICA
licensing@concordtheatricals.co.uk
020-7054-7298

Each title is subject to availability from Concord Theatricals, depending upon country of performance.

CAUTION: Professional and amateur producers are hereby warned that *A SINGLE MAN* is subject to a licensing fee. The purchase, renting, lending or use of this book does not constitute a licence to perform this title(s), which licence must be obtained from the appropriate agent prior to any performance. Performance of this title(s) without a licence is a violation of copyright law and may subject the producer and/or presenter of such performances to penalties. Both amateurs and professionals considering a production are strongly advised to apply to the appropriate agent before starting rehearsals, advertising, or booking a theatre. A licensing fee must be paid whether the title is presented for charity or gain and whether or not admission is charged.

This work is published by Samuel French, an imprint of Concord Theatricals Ltd.

The Professional Rights in this title are held by Berlin Associates, 7 Tyers Gate, Bermondsey, London SE1 3HXS.

No one shall make any changes in this title for the purpose of production. No part of this book may be reproduced, stored in a retrieval system, scanned, uploaded, or transmitted in any form, by any means, now known or yet to be invented, including mechanical, electronic, digital, photocopying, recording, videotaping, or otherwise, without the prior written permission of the publisher. No one shall share this title, or part of this title, to any social media or file hosting websites.

The moral right of Christopher Isherwood and Simon Reade. All Rights Reserved to be identified as author of this work has been asserted in accordance with Section 77 of the Copyright, Designs and Patents Act 1988.

USE OF COPYRIGHTED MUSIC

A licence issued by Concord Theatricals to perform this play does not include permission to use the incidental music specified in this publication. In the United Kingdom: Where the place of performance is already licensed by the PERFORMING RIGHT SOCIETY (PRS) a return of the music used must be made to them. If the place of performance is not so licensed then application should be made to PRS for Music (www.prsformusic.com). A separate and additional licence from PHONOGRAPHIC PERFORMANCE LTD (www.ppluk.com) may be needed whenever commercial recordings are used. Outside the United Kingdom: Please contact the appropriate music licensing authority in your territory for the rights to any incidental music.

USE OF COPYRIGHTED THIRD-PARTY MATERIALS

Licensees are solely responsible for obtaining formal written permission from copyright owners to use copyrighted third-party materials (e.g., artworks, logos) in the performance of this play and are strongly cautioned to do so. If no such permission is obtained by the licensee, then the licensee must use only original materials that the licensee owns and controls. Licensees are solely responsible and liable for clearances of all third-party copyrighted materials, and shall indemnify the copyright owners of the play(s) and their licensing agent, Concord Theatricals Ltd., against any costs, expenses, losses and liabilities arising from the use of such copyrighted third-party materials by licensees.

IMPORTANT BILLING AND CREDIT REQUIREMENTS

If you have obtained performance rights to this title, please refer to your licensing agreement for important billing and credit requirements.

The world premiere production of this adaptation of *A Single Man* opened at Park Theatre on Wednesday, 19 October 2022, produced by Ashley Cook for Troupe Productions Ltd. The cast was as follows:

GEORGE .... Theo Fraser Steele
CHARLEY .... Olivia Darnley
KENNY POTTER / JIM................................ Miles Molan
FEMALE PARAMEDIC / MRS STRUNK / MARIA / DORIS . Phoebe Pryce
MALE PARAMEDIC / MR STRUNK / ALEX / NURSE / BARTENDER .....
.... Freddie Gaminara

Radio Pundits, Students and other roles played by members of the cast.

The performance lasts approximately one hour and fifty minutes including a twenty minute interval.

CREATIVE TEAM

Director	Philip Wilson
Set and Costume Designer	Caitlin Abbott
Lighting Designer	Peter Harrison
Sound Designer and Composer	Beth Duke
Movement Director	Natasha Harrison
Costume Supervisor	Jacqueline Barker
Stage Manager	Alice Wood
Assistant Stage Manager	Helen Parkin-Moore
Production Manager	Ian Taylor
Producer	Ashley Cook

A Single Man is produced by special arrangement with The Wylie Agency (UK) Ltd, 17 Bedford Square, London WC1B 3JA www.wylieagency.com and Berlin Associates, 7 Tyers Gate, London SE1 3HX www.berlinassociates.com

THANKS

George Morgan, Luke Ingram and Elena Frohlick at The Wylie Agency, Marc Berlin, Julia Wyatt, Maddie O'Dwyer and Emily Wraith at Berlin Associates, Jez Bond, Sammie Squire, Dawn James and Matthew Barker at Park Theatre, Robert and Olivia Temple, Dan Dewhirst, Janet Hudson-Holt, Jo Stone-Fewings, George Rowlands, Poppy Miller, Rose Reade, Freddie Gaminara, Rachel Pickup, George Jibson, Amy Reade, Poonamallee Productions, Headlong Theatre, Queen's Theatre, Hornchurch, LAMDA, Stephen and Elizabeth Cook, and Keiron Cooke.

PRODUCTION ACKNOWLEDGEMENTS

Marketing | Richard Fitzmaurice and Alastair Norton for Mobius Industries
Press and PR | Kate Morley and Rebecca Bullamore for Kate Morley PR
Production Image Photography | Michael Wharley Photography
Production Image and Programme Graphic Design | Rebecca Pitt Creative
Publicity, Rehearsal and Production Photography | Mitzi de Margary
Production Insurance | Robert Israel for Gordon & Company
Production Accountancy | Lois Hargreaves for Collins & Company
Bookkeeping | Michelle Brooks

Our patrons are respectfully reminded that, in this intimate theatre, any noise such as rustling programmes, talking or the ringing of mobile phones may distract the actors and your fellow audience-members. We regret there is no admittance or re-admittance to the auditorium whilst the performance is in progress.

PLAYWRIGHT'S NOTES

A SINGLE MAN went through various title options both before – and after – Isherwood's partner, Don Bachardy, gave him his perfect title:

> The Englishwoman
> The Survivor
> Making Do
> A Single Man
> George Is Alone
> He is Alone?
> It Is Alone?

The gestation of the novel can also be charted in Isherwood's *Diaries*, especially in the fall of 1962 in the lead-up to, and aftermath of October's Cuban Missile Crisis.

This dramatisation of *A Single Man* takes its cue from Isherwood's proliferation of theatre and performance metaphors:

– George's kitchen is "an audience of objects – pots and pans, knives and forks, cans and bottles"

– "George is ashamed of his roaring because they aren't play-acting"

– "With the skill of a veteran, he rapidly puts on the psychological makeup for this role he must play"

– "He feels an upsurge of energy, of eagerness for the play to begin"

– "George should be on stage every second, in full control of his performance!"

– George has "a deeply-rooted dramatic instinct...makes his entrance...a subtly contrived, outrageously theatrical effect...like a magician"

– "A performer at the circus has no theatre-curtain to come down and hide him and thus preserve the magic spell of his act unbroken. Poised high on the trapeze under the blazing arcs, he has flashed and pulsed like a star indeed. But now, grounded, unsparkling, unfollowed by spotlights yet plainly visible to anyone who cares to look at him – they are all watching the clowns – he hurries past the tiers of seats toward the exit. Nobody applauds him any more. Very few spare him a single glance"

– "The play has begun now."

The play seeks to match the sensitive poetry, the social, political and mystical vision, and the heart-wrenching drama of the story, with a theatrical flare:

"He is all actor now; an actor on his way up from the dressing-room, hastening through the backstage world of props and lamps and stagehands to make his entrance."

George invents himself before our very eyes, from the naked man who is existentially 'born' in his bed at the start, "I am here now"; to the naked man whose life 'ends' in the very same bed at the finish – his day-in-the-life a life-in-the-day: "The lights go out and there is total blackness." And yet he also starts and finishes with the agony and the ecstasy of bodily functions: pissing; masturbating.

An ensemble revolves around George. He starts and finishes the play, thus retaining the wry, raging, lustful, bitter, luminescent third-person narrative voice of the novel in button-holing asides and Platonic dialogues with himself. Full theatrical weight is given to the rich observations and *cris de coeur* of the novel, hearing Isherwood's voice loud and clear.

So the adaptation plays to the inherent theatricality of the story as it translates to its new medium. The lunacy of the world – in the immediate aftermath of the Cuban Missile Crisis – means that naturalism and social realism can never be mundane ever again. Yet behind the moral and spiritual dimension there is also a matter-of-fact, happens-to-be insouciance in the playing style which can match Isherwood's groundbreaking dramatisation of the life of an outsider: a single, ageing, homosexual, ex-pat Englishman in Southern California in the early 1960s.

Simon Reade, October 2022

THANKS

Maddie O'Dwyer, Emily Wraith, Julia Wyatt and Marc Berlin at Berlin Associates. Luke Ingram at the Wylie Agency. Don Bachardy and Kate Bucknell. Freddie Gaminara, George Jibson, Poppy Miller, Amy Reade, Rose Reade, George Rowlands, Jo Stone-Fewings, Philip Wilson and Ashley Cook. Poonamallee Productions; Troupe Productions.

CHARACTERS

The play can be performed by a cast of as few as five:
GEORGE – (Geo, pronounced Jee-oh), 58
CHARLEY – (Charlotte), 45
KENNY POTTER – (Kenneth), 20 / **JIM**
FEMALE PARAMEDIC / MRS STRUNK – 30s / **MARIA / DORIS** – 20s
MALE PARAMEDIC / MR STRUNK – (Brad) 35 / **ALEX / NURSE / BARTENDER**

SETTING

In the Santa Monica shore region of California, USA.

TIME

The play takes place over 24 hours, from dawn one Friday through to dawn Saturday morning.

NOTES ON STAGING

As well as their assigned 'doubling' roles, the cast may also feature as **RADIO PUNDITS, STUDENTS**, and so on. Whether employing multiple role-playing or a cast of thousands, the focus ultimately will be on a single man.

The stage can be as bare as possible to allow for fluidity and physical invention – a bed, a table and chairs, a few props maybe. It can of course look elegant and stylish (like the Tom Ford/Colin Firth 2009 movie); but it can also accumulate the Coke, cars and crud of the tarnished American Dream that George rails against in the novel. For, in the end, what are we but "cousin to the garbage in the container on the back porch."

The actors can be impeccably costumed, in period: November 1962.

The sun, sea and sky-scapes can be exquisitely lit.

The sound design might be subjective at times.

Don Bachardy suggests using music written by people Isherwood knew, with an American feel. For example, from this period, Stravinsky's *Agon* or something from *The Rake's Progress*. Virgil Thomson's *The River*. Copland's *Fanfare for the Common Man*. Bernstein's *Candide*, his second symphony *The Age of Anxiety* – Leonard Bernstein conducting would be a good choice. Or Gershwin's *Rhapsody in Blue*. Or some Ragtime. A piece Isherwood himself played on the piano in adolescence was Schumann's *The Merry Peasant* which may fit in well with the English countryside scene. For the 1960s hits, remember it was the time of Twist. If a licence or permission is unattainable for the songs, the licensee may not use the songs in A SINGLE MAN but should create an original composition in a similar style or use a similar song in the public domain. For further information, please see Music Use Note on page iii.

Each scene should segue into the next wherever possible.

For Ashley

PART ONE

(One Friday in Santa Monica, California, November 1962.)

Scene One – Home

(A 'family' gathers in vigil at the bedside of a loved one: **JIM** *is relaxed, sat on a barstool, in his naval uniform;* **CHARLEY***, worried, is in a peasant blouse and Mexican skirt. She watches the* **PARAMEDICS** *in medical garb attend to* **GEORGE***, who lies asleep in the bed beneath a sheet and blanket.)*

(A heart-monitor bips distantly, reassuringly.)

(Gentle snoring, a heart-beat, like a mother's, and her child's in the womb.)

(A clock ticks.)

(Then the sounds merge and rise like the rush of the ocean, a wave crashing onto the shore, with a scream – of mother, and child as it's born –.)

JIM. Now!

(– An alarm clock rings rudely – **JIM** *and* **CHARLEY** *exit the stage and the* **PARAMEDICS** *step discreetly into the shadows.)*

*(***GEORGE***'s hand emerges from beneath the sheet and fumbles off the alarm – and all sound stops with it.)*

(Then just the twitter of a November dawn in California.)

(After a pause, almost in baby-talk, from beneath the sheet, an English accent:)

GEORGE. AM ... NOW ... *I* AM NOW ... I AM NOW HERE AT HOME. *(Sounding almost teenage don't-want-to-get-up grumpy:)* Now isn't simply *now*. Now is a cold reminder that it's ONE WHOLE DAY LATER THAN YESTERDAY! One *year* later than last year – rendering all nows obsolete, until later – or sooner – IT WILL COME! Somewhere out there – *(Sits up, eyes wide open.)* – Dead Ahead!

(The skeleton crew of **PARAMEDICS** *re-animate* **GEORGE** *and he performs accordingly:)*

PARAMEDIC. Fear tweaks the vagus nerve.

PARAMEDIC. The cortex has taken its place at the central controls – the legs stretch; the lower back arches; the fingers clench and relax –

PARAMEDIC. The entire inter-communication system issues the first general order of the day:

PARAMEDICS. Now, UP!

*(***GEORGE** *levers his body from beneath the sheet: he's in a white T-shirt and boxer shorts. He takes a few steps like a just-born foal, wincing at twinges in his arthritic left knee, testing his arthritic thumbs. He shambles towards the bathroom, where he lifts the toilet seat, and pees – to his evident relief.)*

(He flushes. He steps onto the bathroom scales:)

GEORGE. One hundred and fifty seven pounds?! In spite of all the toiling at the gym!

*(***GEORGE** *shuffles to the mirror and looks in – his accentuated face stares back:)*

(Groucho Marx voice:) That isn't so much a face as the expression of a predicament! Here's the mess it has got itself into during its FIFTY-EIGHT-YEARS!

(He manipulates his features, like rubber.)

PARAMEDIC. He looks desperately tired – but there's no question of stopping! The creature we are watching will struggle on and on until he drops!

*(**GEORGE** stares back into the mirror:)*

GEORGE. So many faces within the face... the child... the boy... the young man... the not-so-young man – preserved like fossils, layers upon Jurassic layers. Withered. Dead.

PARAMEDIC. *(To* **GEORGE.***)* Hey, living-dying creature! What is there to be afraid of?

*(**GEORGE** turns away from the conversation he's having in the mirror and responds:)*

GEORGE. I am afraid of being *rushed*!

(Copland's Fanfare for the Common man might play under:)

PARAMEDIC. Now, wash!

*(**GEORGE** scrubs his face with a cloth.)*

PARAMEDIC. Shave!

*(**GEORGE** applies shaving cream – and whips it off again with a razor.)*

PARAMEDIC. Brush!

*(**GEORGE** brushes his hair. As he does so:)*

GEORGE. *(To himself in the mirror:)* You know you have responsibilities. You know what's expected.

PARAMEDIC. You know your name?

GEORGE. *(Carefully.)* George.

> *(**GEORGE** beams. The **PARAMEDICS** bring on his clothes like valets and transform **GEORGE** from middle-aged slump in his undies – by dressing him in crisp pants (trousers), polished shoes, ironed shirt, neat cuffs and cufflinks, finishing touch with tie and glasses – into an Englishman Abroad, as the brass fanfare climaxes –.)*

(The music cuts out abruptly.)

(More or less satisfied:) More or less George.

> *(The **PARAMEDICS** more or less agree and retreat to the margin.)*

> *(**GEORGE** checks his watch; sees he has plenty of time to take us on a guided tour:)*

This is a tightly planned little house... here is the study – note the couch that transforms into a bed... down the steep, narrow staircase *(He descends.)*, turn the corner *(He turns.)* – you can touch both handrails with your elbows and you have to bend your head *(He demonstrates.)* – Is it on the small side? Well there's hardly room enough to feel lonely. Think of two people, living together, day after day, squeezing past each other on these narrow stairs –

> *(This is choreographed (to a John Cage minimalist piece?) with **JIM**:)*

– jostling, bumping into each other – by mistake, or on purpose – awkwardly, in rage, in love – think what tracks they must leave behind them! Two people in a hurry, *colliding* –

> *(**GEORGE** is brought up short.)*

JIM IS DEAD!

> (**JIM** *departs. The stage feels suddenly cold and bare and empty, apart from* **GEORGE**. *He has a spasm. Then stillness.*)

> (**GEORGE** *composes himself, goes into the kitchen – the shish of a tap, and he glugs a glass of water; the whoomph! of the gas as it's lit; the sizzle of a frying-pan.*)

> (*In the sing-song falsetto of his Nanny:*)

POACHED EGGS ON TOAST ARE VERY NICE
IF YOU TRY THEM ONCE YOU'LL WANT THEM TWICE!

– Oh, Nanny! If only all *was* safe in our dear, tiny, doomed world! Breakfast with Jim used to be one of the best times of the day. On our second – no, *third* cup of coffee – we'd have our best talks. About everything that came into our heads. Including death, of course:

> (**JIM** *appears again from the shadows, observing* **GEORGE**, *real to* **GEORGE**:)

(*To (the imaginary)* **JIM**:) If there is survival, then what exactly is it that *survives*? Better to be killed instantly? Or to know you're about to die?... I can't for the life of me remember what you thought... suppose the dead do revisit the living? Would you return to see how I was getting along? What would you see? A solitary figure sat at a small table, eating poached eggs, a prisoner for life.

> (**JIM** *retreats again.*)

> (**GEORGE** *continues with the tour:*)

Here's the living-room. D'you admire all the books? They haven't made me noble or better or truly *wise*. I just like listening to their voices.

> (*A cacophony of literary babbling.*)

One at a time!

(The clock ticks.)

Some put me to sleep; some take my mind off the ticking hands of the clock; some gossip me out of my melancholy day.

(He takes one off the shelf at random:)

Ah, Ruskin: always absolutely in the right, and crazy, and so cross, with his whiskers, scolding the English – *(Of Ruskin and the book:)* the perfect companion for five minutes on the toilet!

*(**GEORGE** returns to the toilet, pulls down his pants, and squats, reading. Then looks up:)*

Sitting on the john, I can look out of the window – my neighbours can see my head and shoulders from across the street, but not what I'm doing.

*(He waves at his neighbours **MR STRUNK** and **MRS STRUNK** – they wave cheerily back.)*

(Cod hard-boiled Chandleresque accent:) It was a grey, lukewarm, California winter morning; the sky low and soft with Pacific fog... *(In his own voice:)* This street is called Camphor Tree Lane. Maybe Camphor trees grew here once? *(Shrugs.)* More probably the name was chosen for its picturesqueness by the pioneer escapists from dingy downtown Los Angeles, who came out here and founded this colony back in the twenties – as a last-ditch stand against the twentieth century:

PIONEER ESCAPIST NEIGHBOUR (MRS STRUNK). Thank heavens we have escaped the soul-destroying commercialisation of the city!

*(**GEORGE** smiles.)*

GEORGE. They were tacky and cheerful and defiantly bohemian – and boundlessly tolerant. When they fought, it was with fists and bottles, not lawyers. Then, in the late forties, the World War Two Vets came swarming out of the East with their just-married wives, in search of new and better breeding-grounds:

WORLD WAR TWO VET (MR STRUNK). Hey! Hillside neighbourhood? Check. Five minutes walk from the beach? Check. No through traffic to decimate our future tots? What's not to like!

    (**GEORGE** *cringes.*)

GEORGE. Breeding and bohemianism do not mix. So the cottages that used to reek of gin and poetry fell to the occupying army of Coca-Cola-drinking television-watchers. For breeding you need a steady job, a mortgage, you need credit, insurance – and don't you dare die until the family's future is provided for! Tots appeared – litter after litter. The pokey old schoolhouse became a group of airy new school-buildings. The shabby market on the ocean front transformed into a *super*-market with parking lot round the back. And on Camphor Tree Lane, two signs were posted:

MR STRUNK. *(Through a loud-hailer.)* Do not eat the watercress!

    (*Everyone stops, stares questioningly at* **MR STRUNK**: *say what?* – **MR STRUNK** *explains:*)

It grows along the bed of the creek and the water is polluted.

    (*Gotcha, they nod.*)

GEORGE. And the other sign? Sinister, black silhouettes on a yellow background:

    (*Cue 1940s film noir climax, da-da-DAH!*)

MR STRUNK. *(Through loud-hailer.)* CHILDREN AT PLAY!

(The Psycho violin shriek and Edvard Munch Scream faces of everyone but **GEORGE**, *fleeing the stage.)*

GEORGE. What can I say? We fell in love-at-first-sight with the house. We loved it because you can only get to it across the bridge over the creek – as good as being on our own island! *(To* **MR STRUNK**, *off:)* And the watercress is delicious! The bridge was beginning to sag a little – but Jim said he expected it would last out our time…

(Outside a trash can clatters, a cat miaaaoows!, a dog woofs, a kid, **BENNY**, *off, cackles.)*

MRS STRUNK. *(Half off, half on the phone.)* Hey, Benny, leave the Professor alone! He's, you know, sad. *(She resumes her phone conversation:)* Benny's going through his Aggressive Phase – *(Proud:)* right on schedule! Couldn't be more normal and healthy.

*(***BENNY**, *off, smashes something electrical with a hammer.)*

(To **BENNY**:*)* Benny! Put it back in the trash can, now!

(It sounds like **BENNY** *does as he's told.)*

(Half to **BENNY**, *half into phone:)* Atta-boy!

GEORGE. And then the fathers with their jobs – nerves frayed, tempers uncertain –

*(***MR STRUNK** *re-enters, frazzled.* **BENNY**, *off, starts hammering the trash can again.)*

MR STRUNK. Hey, Benny! NO MORE NOISE!

GEORGE. – But they're proud of their families, glad of their jobs –

MR STRUNK. *(Grinning as if for a portrait.)* Co-Owner of the American Utopia, the Kingdom of the Good Life Upon Earth –

GEORGE. *(Ironic.)* Crudely aped by the Russians, hated by the Chinese –

MR STRUNK. *(Hand on heart:)* We pledge to starve ourselves for generations in the hopeless hope of inheriting that Kingdom!

GEORGE. But Mr Strunk – like his son Benny, like his wife Mrs Strunk, like all the rest of them – he is afraid: because somewhere in the darkness is a fiend who won't fit the stats, a bad-smelling beast that doesn't use their deodorants, the unspeakable that insists on speaking its name – Me! They are afraid of little old me!

MR STRUNK. He's a queer!

MRS STRUNK. *(To her husband:)* Shush!

MR STRUNK. – Not that I give a damn what he gets up to in the privacy of his own… just as long as he stays away from me and mine!

GEORGE. Oh, Mr Strunk! Those photographs of you in the college football team?

> *(**MR STRUNK** poses again, cheesily for his College football team photo.)*

You were a living doll!

> *(**MR STRUNK** winks at **GEORGE**.)*

MRS STRUNK. *(To her husband.)* It's all due to heredity, and their early environment. Shame on those possessive mothers and those sex-segregated British schools! *(Nonetheless she calls **BENNY** in, protectively:)* Benny! You come in now! It's not safe to play outside, alone.

> *(**BENNY** clearly obeys, as a trash can lid clatters.)*

MR STRUNK. *(To his wife.)* You read too many of those goddamn psychology books!

MRS STRUNK. It's arrested development. Imagine being a misfit! Pity the Professor; don't *blame* him. *(Quoting from her psychology book:)* Some cases, caught early enough, *may* respond to treatment. As for the rest – *(Looking at* **GEORGE.***)* ah, it's so sad. Especially when it happens to someone truly worthwhile who has so much to offer. Some of them are geniuses, you know; but their masterpieces are...

MR STRUNK. Warped?

MRS STRUNK. Well, there were the Greeks – but they were pagans, not neurotics. And nowadays they know that, when in a relationship, it's just a substitute for... take the Professor and young Jim.

MR STRUNK. Whatever happened to the boy Jim? Nice-looking young fella.

MRS STRUNK. *(Of* **GEORGE.***)* Poor old man, living there all alone. He has such a kind face.

GEORGE. She doesn't know what happened to Jim, none of them do – Jim is never coming back from Ohio, where it happened – I simply spread it about that Jim's folks, who are getting on in years, persuaded their son to come home and live with them – where he will remain indefinitely. As for Jim's *animals*, I had to get rid of them – devilish reminders... *(To* **MRS STRUNK,** *off:)* Your book is wrong, Mrs Strunk, when it tells you Jim is the substitute for a real son, a kid brother. *Jim wasn't a substitute for anything!*

*(***GEORGE***'s phone rings.)*

Damn!

*(***GEORGE** *pulls up his underwear, shuffles as swiftly as he can to his study, trousers at half-mast like a man in a sack-race, answers the urgently ringing phone.)*

Hello?

CHARLEY. *(English but Californified accent.)* Geo? It *is* you!

> (**CHARLOTTE***'s voice / split-stage.*)

GEORGE. Hello, Charley.

CHARLEY. I didn't call too early, did I? I was afraid, if I'd waited longer, you'd have already gone to the College – my goodness, I hadn't noticed it was so late! Oughtn't you to be there already?

GEORGE. *(Patient.)* This is my one-class day, which doesn't start until eleven. You remember: my early days are Mondays and Wednesdays.

CHARLEY. Oh yes, of course!

> *(Pause.* **GEORGE** *looks at his watch; waits for the inevitable request from* **CHARLEY***:)*

Geo...

GEORGE. Yes, Charley.

CHARLEY. Would you possibly be free tonight?

GEORGE. *(Immediate, abrupt.)* Afraid not. No.

CHARLEY. Oh – I see... It *is* short notice...

> (**GEORGE***'s face is puckered in a grimace of guilt and discomfort.)*

I suppose you couldn't – I mean – I suppose it's something important?

GEORGE. I'm afraid it is.

CHARLEY. I see... oh well, never mind. *(Brave:)* I'll try you again in a few days?

GEORGE. Of course. *(Relenting a little.)* Or I'll call you.

CHARLEY. *(Brightens.)* Oh, would you?

(Pause.)

Well, goodbye, Geo.

GEORGE. Goodbye, Charley.

(They both hang up. **CHARLOTTE** *disappears.)*

(A hit song of summer of 1962 starts up and builds under:)

*(***GEORGE*** pulls up his trousers, flushes the toilet, grabs his jacket, chucks his lecture notes and his copy of Aldous Huxley's* After Many A Summer *into his briefcase, swipes his car keys, opens the front door – where* **MRS STRUNK** *is about to press the doorbell just as he opens the door:)*

Mrs Strunk!

(The music abruptly stops.)

MRS STRUNK. *(Nervous.)* Oh, good morning – I – we have been meaning to ask – I know how busy you are – but we haven't gotten together in such a long while – and we were wondering – would-you-possibly-have-time-tonight-to-come-for-a-drink-it'll-just-be-the-two-of-us-at-home?

GEORGE. I'm most terribly sorry. I'm afraid I planned on being out.

MRS STRUNK. Oh. Well. I was afraid you wouldn't have time –

GEORGE. *(Surprised, touched.)* No, listen. I really *would* like it. Do you suppose I could take a rain-check?

MRS STRUNK. *(Sceptical.)* Well, yes, of course –

GEORGE. *(Trying to convince.)* I would *love* to come. How about tomorrow?

MRS STRUNK. *(Face falls in mortification.)* Oh well, tomorrow. Tomorrow wouldn't be so good, I'm afraid. Tomorrow we have some *friends* coming over from the Valley and they wouldn't…

GEORGE. *(Not wanting to embarrass her.)* I understand, of course; but let's make it very soon, shall we?

MRS STRUNK. *(Fervently.)* Oh *yes, very* soon –

> *(She scuttles away.* **GEORGE** *goes to the car, gets in, is about to shut the car door –.)*

MR STRUNK. *(Offstage.)* What did he say?

MRS STRUNK. *(Offstage.)* He says no. He's got a date.

MR STRUNK. *(Offstage.)* Faggot.

MRS STRUNK. *(Offstage.)* Brad! I feel sorry for him…

> *(As* **GEORGE** *slams shut the car door, the scene slam cuts to:)*

Scene Two – Freeway

*(**GEORGE** is driving on the freeway, content. The hit summer of '62 song is now tinnily playing on the car radio.)*

GEORGE. *(Like a public service infomercial:)* It is one of the marvels of the Los Angeles freeway system that you can get from the beach to San Tomas State College in fifty minutes! *(Himself:)* Give or take five. I feel a kind of patriotism for the freeways – proud that they are so fast. I *love* them because I can still cope with them. The fact that I can *cope* proves that I am a functioning member of society. I can still *get by*.

(He tenses up for the car race:)

Here in the midst of the mad metropolitan chariot race – Ben Hur would certainly chicken out – jockeying from lane to lane with the best of them – never getting rattled when a crazy teenager hangs on your tail – when a woman cuts in sharply ahead of you – that's what comes of letting them go first through doorways! – Never dropping below eighty, in the fast lane –

(Honk!)

Rage! Such is the vitality of middle age!

*(Then **GEORGE** visibly relaxes, shoulders un-hunch, body easing back.)*

(In Yoga guru voice:) Think of this not as a mad chariot race but as a river, sweeping full flood towards the crest of the pass, the Valley stretched out ahead under a long brown smear of smog, beyond and above which the big barren mountains rise...

(He turns the dial on the car radio – pre-record/live:)

RADIO PUNDIT #1. ...a high-rise on the edge of the beach? It will block the view! And they call that progress?!

*(**GEORGE** retunes.)*

RADIO PUNDIT #2. ...we should attack Cuba right now! With everything we've got! So what if the Russians attack us back? We must prepare to sacrifice three quarters of our population...

*(**GEORGE** retunes.)*

RADIO PUNDIT #3. ... Sex deviates! They are everywhere. You can't go into a bar anymore, or a men's room, or a public library. And they all, without exception, have syphilis. The existing laws against them are far too lenient!

*(The **RADIO** chunters on.)*

GEORGE. Everyone responsible for peddling the myth of sex deviates should be kidnapped and taken to some secret underground movie studio, where they'd be encouraged to perform every possible sex act – which they would all utterly enjoy – and then we'd release the movie under the title COMING ATTRACTIONS!

(He twists the dial back to music – looks up.)

Downtown already! In ten minutes George will have to be George – the George they recognise – so, start thinking their thoughts!

(A new, busy song erupts on the radio and takes us into:)

Scene Three – Campus

(**GEORGE** *strides across Campus to the loud music which started on the radio, towards the lecture hall, amidst a swirl of choreographed, dancing* **STUDENTS**:)

GEORGE. Behold the male and female raw material which is daily fed into this factory to be processed, all hurrying in pursuit of their shedules-skedules, all book-burdened, harassed, preparing themselves… for life, for a job and security in which to raise children, to prepare them in turn… for life, for a job and security in which to raise children, to prepare them in turn –

(The musical number coasts.)

But despite all the advice about what good money they'll earn in pharmacology, or accountancy, or electronics, there are still, incredibly, quite a few who persist in writing poems, and novels, and plays! Goofy from lack of sleep, they scribble in snatched moments, their brains dizzy with words. Will any of them make it? Oh, sure. One at least. In all these searching thousands. And what will become of all the rest? Ought they to know it is hopeless?

But I am the representative of their hope. I am the one who made it.

(He is all actor now – makes his entrance:)

(Boldly, clearly:) Good morning!

STUDENTS. Good morning!

(One **STUDENT**, **KENNY**, *makes his grinning conspicuous entrance a beat late.)*

KENNY. Good morning, sir!

GEORGE. Good morning, Kenny – good, despite the Russians and their rockets. Good, despite all the ills of the flesh. Good to be in America, where worries can be *un*thought and made to vanish!

> *(The faculty bell rings: eleven a.m. – a drum roll...)*

Scene Four – Lecture

> *(... Drum roll... the* **STUDENTS** *hurriedly take their place in the front row of the auditorium in eager expectation –* **KENNY**, *grinning, charmingly pulling focus...)*

> *(...Drum rolling,* **GEORGE**, *the magician, pulls a rabbit from a hat (the book from his briefcase) – cymbal crash!)*

GEORGE. "After many a summer *dies* the swan."

> *(Dramatic pause.* **GEORGE** *takes in his audience.)*

(Ironic, school-masterish tone) I take it you've all read the Huxley novel, seeing as I asked you to three weeks ago?

> *(The* **STUDENTS** *are variously embarrassed that they haven't/affronted that they were never told/keen to beam that indeed they have.)*

The title is, of course, a quotation from Tennyson's poem *Tithonus*. And who was Tithonus?

> *(He looks from blank face to blank face.)*

You seriously mean to tell me that none of you know? That none of you could be bothered to find out? Then I advise you all to spend your weekend reading Robert Graves's *Greek Myths* – and the poem itself. *(Ill-tempered)* I don't see how anyone can pretend to be interested in a novel when they don't even stop to ask themselves what its title means. Well, to begin at the beginning...

> *(The following trips off the tongue in a dazzling performance, acted out as it goes.)*

Aphrodite once caught her lover Ares in bed with Eos, goddess of Dawn. Aphrodite was furious – so she cursed Eos with a craze for handsome mortal boys, to teach her to *(With comic petulance and even a foot-stamp.)* Leave Other People's Gods Alone!

(Giggles.)

Eos was terribly embarrassed, but found she just couldn't help herself, so she started seducing and then kidnapping boys from Earth. Tithonus was one of them. As a matter of fact, she took his brother Ganymede along too, for company.

(Louder giggles.)

Unfortunately, Zeus saw Ganymede and fell madly in love with him.

(Giggles of delight.)

So, knowing that she'd have to give up Ganymede anyway, Eos asked Zeus if, in exchange for Ganymede, he'd make Tithonus immortal? So Zeus said: "Of course, why not?" But Eos was so stupid, she forgot to ask him to give Tithonus eternal youth.

(Laughter.)

So poor Tithonus gradually became a repulsively immortal old man.

(Loud laughter.)

And Eos, with the characteristic heartlessness of a goddess, got bored with him and locked him up. And he got more and more gaga, and his voice got shriller and shriller, until one day he turned into... a cicada.

(Silence in the auditorium. A distant thrum of cicadas from outside.)

(Briskly, authoritatively:) Huxley's general reason for choosing this title is obvious. But before we can go any further, you've got to make up your minds what this novel is actually *about*.

> *(He looks expectantly at his audience, looking from face to face.)*
>
> *(Eventually* **ALEX** *raises his hand.)*

Yes. Alex.

ALEX. *(Californian drawl.)* It's about this rich guy who's jealous because he's afraid he's too old for this girl, and he thinks this young guy is on the make for her, only he isn't, and he doesn't have a hope, because she and the doctor already made the scene, so the rich guy shoots the young guy by mistake, and the doctor like covers up for them, and then they all go to England to find this Earl character who's monkeying around with a dame in a cellar –

> *(A roar of joy.* **GEORGE** *smiles good-sportingly.)*

GEORGE. You left out Mr Propter and Mr Pordage.

ALEX. Pordage? Oh yeah – he's the one that finds out about the Earl eating the crazy fish –

GEORGE. Carp.

ALEXANDER. That's right...

GEORGE. And Propter?

ALEX. *(Scratching his head, clowning it up.)* I'm sorry, sir. You'll just have to excuse me. I mean I didn't hit the sack till like half-past two this morning, trying to figure that cat out. Wow! I don't dig that jazz.

> *(More laughter. Then the following chipped in by from* **STUDENTS***/pre-records, overlapping.)*

STUDENTS. – Mr Propter shouldn't have said the ego is unreal; this proves he has no faith in human nature;

– It teaches us that we aren't meant to pry into the mysteries of life; we mustn't tamper with eternity;

– This novel is arid and abstract mysticism; what do we need eternity for anyway?

– Mr Huxley is marvellously zany;

–To say time is evil because evil happens in time is like saying the ocean is a fish because fish happen in the ocean;

– Mr Propter has no sex life; this makes him unconvincing as a character;

– Mr Huxley really understands women; giving Virginia a rose-coloured motor scooter is a perfect touch –

*(Then **MARIA** chips in:)*

MARIA. Sir, here on page seventy nine, Mr Propter says the stupidest text in the Bible is "They hated me without cause". Does he mean by that the Nazis were right to hate the Jews? Is Huxley anti-Semitic?

*(Silence. **GEORGE** draws a long breath. Then he starts, mildly:)*

GEORGE. No. Mr Huxley is not anti-Semitic. The Nazis were *not* right to hate the Jews. Let's think about this in terms of some other minority. For example, people with freckles aren't thought of as a minority by the non-freckled. They aren't a minority in the sense we're talking about. And why aren't they? Because a minority is only thought of as a minority when it contributes some kind of threat to the majority – real or imaginary.

(He's off again, increasingly talking about himself rather than an abstract minority, or specifically Jewish people.)

Now along come the liberals – which includes everybody in this room, I trust – and they say "minorities are just like us." Sure, minorities are people; *people*, not angels. Sure, they're like us – but not *exactly* like us. A minority has its own kind of aggression. It may hate the majority – not without cause, I grant you. It may even hate other minorities – because all minorities are in competition, each one may claim its sufferings are worse than another's sufferings. And the more they hate, and the more they're persecuted, the nastier they can become! While you're being persecuted, you hate what's happening to you, you hate the people who are making it happen; you're in a world of hate. And if someone reaches out to you? Well, you suspect love! You think there's something behind it – some motive – some trick –

> *(The bell for the end of the lecture, Noon, sounds rudely. Everyone stirs.)*

– We'll carry on with this on Monday.

> *(They all rise instantly to their feet.* **GEORGE***'s feathers remain ruffled.)*

> *(***MARIA*** and* **ALEX** *line up to ask questions – partly to impress themselves upon him, partly flirtatious –* **KENNY** *hangs back.)*

Yes, Maria.

MARIA. When you set the final examination, will you require us to have read *all* the books Mr Huxley mentions in his novel?

GEORGE. *(Teasing.)* Including *The 120 Days of Sodom*?

MARIA. Professor?

GEORGE. Not all. Just the ones that rouse your curiosity.

MARIA. Thank you, sir. My academic load will be much lighter.

(She leaves, relieved.)

GEORGE. *(To the next.)* Yes, Alex.

ALEX. I'm sorry, sir. I didn't read *all* the Huxley because I thought you'd be going through it with us first.

*(**GEORGE** chooses to ignore this sly idiocy and admire **ALEX**'s button-badge instead.)*

GEORGE. Ban the Bomb!

ALEX. Yes, sir, you bet!

*(**ALEX** departs, satisfied. **MARIA** returns.)*

MARIA. Do you think Mr Huxley had an actual English village in mind?

GEORGE. I don't know, Maria. All I can say with some certainty is that in the last chapter they appear to be driving out of London in a south-westerly direction. So, most likely, it's meant to be somewhere in Hampshire...

MARIA. I spent three unforgettable weeks in England ten years ago, mainly in Scotland. And a short while in London. Whenever you're speaking to us, I keep remembering that beautiful accent. It's like music.

GEORGE. Cockney or Gorbals?

*(**MARIA** is uncomprehending.)*

MARIA. Where was your birthplace?

GEORGE. Cheshire.

MARIA. Cheshire? I have never heard of that!

*(**GEORGE** sweeps out – but is waylaid by the last, grinning **STUDENT**, **KENNY**:)*

KENNY. Sir!

GEORGE. Kenny. What do you want to know?

KENNY. Did you ever take mescaline, sir, like Huxley?

GEORGE. Huxley wasn't a dope addict.

KENNY. No, sir. But did you? Ever?

GEORGE. Yes, once. In New York. About eight years ago. There weren't any regulations against selling it, then. I just went into a drugstore and bought some.

KENNY. And did it make you see things – like mystical visions and stuff?

GEORGE. Not what you'd call visions. At first I felt seasick. And a bit scared, of course. Like Dr. Jekyll might have felt after he'd taken his drug for the first time…

> *(**KENNY** doesn't register the literary/popular reference, just keeps grinning. The lights and sound and atmosphere subtly change to reflect the following experience:)*

And then certain colours began to get very bright and stand out. You wondered why everybody didn't notice them. And people's faces turn into caricatures – I mean you seem to see what each one is about. One is absurdly vain; another is worrying himself sick; another longs to pick a fight. Then you see a very few who are simply beautiful because they aren't anxious or aggressive about anything; they take life as it comes. And then, while the thing is working its full strength, it's as if the walls of the room and everything around you is breathing… and then it all slowly dies down again, back to normal.

> *(An inhalation, an exhalation, like a wave – then the atmosphere returns to normal.)*

Afterwards I felt fine. I ate a huge supper.

KENNY. You didn't take it again?

GEORGE. No. I didn't want to, particularly. It was just an experience I'd had. I gave the rest of the capsules to friends –

KENNY. You don't have any of those capsules left now, do you, sir?

GEORGE. No, Kenny, I do not! And even if I did, I wouldn't distribute them to students. I can think of far more amusing ways of getting myself thrown out of this place.

KENNY. Sorry, sir. I was only wondering… I guess, if I really wanted the stuff, I could get it easily enough, right here on campus. This friend of Lois, *he* claims when he took it, he saw God.

GEORGE. Maybe he did. Maybe I just didn't take enough.

KENNY. *(Amused.)* You know something, sir? I bet, even if you *had* seen God, you wouldn't tell us.

GEORGE. What makes you say that?

KENNY. It's what Lois says.

GEORGE. Lois is your girlfriend?

KENNY. Kind of.

GEORGE. Lois from my class?

    (**KENNY** *nods.*)

KENNY. She thinks you're – well, kind of cagey. Like just now, listening to all that crap we were talking about Huxley –

GEORGE. I didn't notice *you* doing much talking!

KENNY. I was watching you… I think Lois is right! You let us ramble on, and then you straighten us out, and I'm not saying you don't teach us a lot of interesting stuff – you do – but you never tell us *all* you know about something –

GEORGE. *(Flattered, excited, slipping into the role.)* Well – maybe that's true, up to a point... you see, Kenny, there are some things you don't even *know* you know, until you're asked.

KENNY. *(Matter-of-fact.)* I have to go down to the bookstore.

GEORGE. OK.

> *(They walk off together,* **KENNY** *grinning...)*

Scene Five – Kenny

(... Continuous, as they stroll across campus:)

*(As they reach the tennis courts, **GEORGE** is momentarily distracted by **ALEX** playing at one end, **MARIA** at the other, both sweaty but idealised physical specimens of youth:)*

(Phut – Tok! – Phut – Tok! – Phut – Tok! – 15 Love!)

GEORGE. *(To **KENNY**, meaningfully.)* Someone has to ask you a question before you can answer it. It's seldom you find anyone who'll ask the right questions. Most people aren't that interested –

> *(**KENNY** stares at **GEORGE**, smiling – but not asking. **GEORGE** averts his gaze and looks at the ground, tries to keep things impersonal.)*

It's not that I *want* to be cagey. So often I feel I want to *tell* things, *discuss* things, *absolutely frankly*. I don't mean in class of course. Someone would be sure to misunderstand –

*(Silence. **GEORGE** looks up.)*

KENNY. *(Abruptly.)* Maybe this friend of Lois's didn't see God, after all? I mean, not long after he took the stuff, he had a breakdown. He told Lois that while he was locked up for three months in the institution, he turned into the Devil. He said the police had a machine for catching devils and liquidating them. It was called a MO-machine – MO, that's OM – you know, the Indian word for God? – spelled backwards?

GEORGE. If the police liquidated devils, that would mean they were angels, wouldn't it?

> *(**KENNY** grins and nods.)*

Makes sense. A place where police are angels has to be an insane asylum.

> (**KENNY** *laughs loudly – NB when* **KENNY** *laughs his deep rather wild laugh,* **GEORGE** *sometimes feels he is being laughed at. When the laugh comes a fraction of a moment late,* **GEORGE** *gets a spooky impression that* **KENNY** *is laughing not at the joke but at the whole situation – the educational system, the economic and political and psychological forces which have brought them all together on this campus.)*

(They have arrived at the bookstore.)

Here we are. The bookshop.

KENNY. I don't need a book. I need a pencil sharpener.

> *(***KENNY*** buys a red pencil sharpener.)*

What was it you wanted to get, sir?

GEORGE. Well, nothing, actually.

KENNY. You mean, you walked all the way down here just to keep me company?

GEORGE. Sure. Why not?

KENNY. *(Sincerely surprised and pleased.)* Well, I think you deserve something for that! Here. Choose a pencil sharpener. It's on me!

GEORGE. Oh – well – thank you!

> *(***GEORGE*** chooses a yellow one.* **KENNY** *grins.)*

KENNY. I kind of expected you to pick blue.

GEORGE. Why?

KENNY. Isn't blue supposed to be spiritual?

GEORGE. What makes you think I want to be spiritual? And how come you picked red?

KENNY. What's red stand for?

GEORGE. Rage. And lust.

KENNY. No kidding?

> *(They grin at one another, in silence, almost intimately.)*

You know those courses for police students?

> *(**GEORGE** nods.)*

Today a special man from Washington is addressing them on twenty ways to spot a commie.

GEORGE. No kidding!

KENNY. Do you want to go? We might ask some awkward questions!

GEORGE. What time?

KENNY. Three o'clock.

GEORGE. *(Regretfully.)* I can't. I've got to be downtown in an hour... the hospital. I'm visiting a... friend. A young friend.

KENNY. Too bad.

GEORGE. Too bad.

> *(Then **KENNY** waves a casual dismissal.)*

KENNY. See you around.

> *(**KENNY** strolls away. **GEORGE** watches after him.)*
>
> *(A heart-monitor bips distantly. **GEORGE** checks his watch – walks off with purpose to...)*

Scene Six – Hospital

> *(Heart monitors. The distant tannoy call of "Doctor Perera to the operating theatre, Doctor Perera to the operating theatre, please":)*
>
> *(**GEORGE** checks his watch again. The shoosh of automatic doors. **GEORGE** is momentarily fearful of stepping across the threshold. Nonetheless, he steps in.)*
>
> *(Lights fade up on **DORIS**: in her twenties, but shrivelled and emaciated, lying in bed, facing the window, sunlight shafting through the louvered blinds.)*
>
> *(**GEORGE** looks at her with pity.)*
>
> *(The clock ticks: two fifty one p.m.)*
>
> *(**DORIS** turns towards **GEORGE**.)*

DORIS. Hello?

GEORGE. Hello, Doris.

> *(**GEORGE** sits on the edge of her bed, takes her hand:)*

We are on the same road, you and I. I shall follow you soon.

> *(**DORIS** smiles faintly.)*

DORIS. I made such a noise, yesterday. *(To herself:)* Was it yesterday? *(To **GEORGE**:)* I was screaming. They had to fetch the doctor.

> *(**DORIS** smiles.)*

GEORGE. Was it your back?

DORIS. What time is it?

GEORGE. Nearly three o'clock.

> *(A long silence.)*

I was on the pier the other day. I hadn't been there in ages. And, do you know, they've torn down the old roller-skating rink? It seems as if they can't bear to leave anything the way it used to be. Do you remember the booth where the woman used to read your character from your handwriting? That's gone too –

> *(He stops short, dismayed –.)*

It was while Jim and I were roller-skating that we first met you – you were with a boy named Norman – you quickly ditched him. And later we all had our handwriting read. Do you remember?

> *(A long silence. The clock ticks.)*

DORIS. What did you say the time was?

GEORGE. Nearly three. Four minutes of.

DORIS. Look into the corridor, will you? See if anyone's there.

> *(**GEORGE** gets up, goes to the door – before he's even reached the door she asks with harsh impatience:)*

Well?

GEORGE. *(Looking out into corridor.)* No one there.

DORIS. *(Desperate.)* Where's the fucking nurse?

GEORGE. Shall I go and see?

DORIS. They know I get a shot at three. They don't give a shit.

GEORGE. I'll find them.

DORIS. Bitch won't come till they're good and ready.

GEORGE. I'm sure I can find –

DORIS. No! Stay here.

GEORGE. Okay.

DORIS. Sit down again.

GEORGE. Sure.

> (**GEORGE** *obliges. He holds out his hand again; she grips it with astonishing strength.*)

DORIS. George –

GEORGE. Yes?

DORIS. You'll stay till they come?

GEORGE. Of course I will.

> (**DORIS**'s *grip tightens.*)

> (*The* **NURSE** *appears in the doorway, smiling, with a tray full of hypodermics.*)

NURSE. I'm punctual today, see!

GEORGE. *(Rising at once.)* I'll be going.

NURSE. Oh, you don't have to do that. This won't take any time at all.

GEORGE. I have to go anyway.

NURSE. She's been a bad girl. We can't get her to eat her lunch, can we?

GEORGE. Well, so long, Doris. See you again in a couple of days.

DORIS. *(Not looking at him – eyes on the needle)* Goodbye, George.

> (**GEORGE** *goes – he looks back on the scene:*)

GEORGE. *(To himself.)* Did she *mean* Goodbye? What has this young, dying woman, with these sticks of arms and legs – what has she to do with that big animal of a girl who, momentarily, stole Jim from me? Would I ever, even then, have wished this on her?

(To **JIM.***)* You would be appalled if you could see her now, Jim. I've stopped bringing her flowers, you know, bringing her gifts. I no longer see the point. She is now just absorbed in the business of dying.

You used to complain and raise hell over a head-cold, a grazed finger. But you were lucky at the end…

(To himself.) The truck hit his car just right; he never felt it. They never even got to take him to a place like this. He was dead at the scene.

How good to be in a body – *(He touches his chest.)* even this old beat-up carcass. It still has warm blood, rich marrow, wholesome flesh! It has outlived Jim; it will outlive Doris. I am alive!

> *(A shopping trolley wheels on,* **GEORGE** *grabs it and steps into:)*

Scene Seven – Supermarket

(A living death. Brilliantly illuminated. Christmas Muzak.)

*(**GEORGE**, wheels the shopping-trolley along the aisles.)*

GEORGE. *(To himself.)* Christmas, already?! Jeez. Maybe I'll do something *drastic* this Christmas; take a 'plane to Mexico City and be drunk for a week and run wild... You won't; you never will...

(He takes something off a shelf, places it in his trolley.)

Hardly more than a month ago, before Khrushchev agreed to pull his rockets out of Cuba, we were cramming our shopping baskets, buying the shelves bare of beans and rice. Now look at us – so much to choose from!

You could spend hours of your life in here. Shimmering brands in shiny boxes – 'take me, take me!' – but when you get them back to your empty room, all that remains is cardboard and cellophane... Ambushed by bottles and cans with shockingly vivid memories of meals shopped for, cooked, and eaten with Jim. Who says I have to be brave? Who depends on me now? Who cares? Damn all food! Damn all life!

*(**GEORGE** makes a decision, makes a bee-line for the payphone. Inserts his dime. Dials.)*

CHARLEY. Hello?

(Voice only / Split-stage.)

GEORGE. Hello, Charley.

CHARLEY. Geo –!

GEORGE. Listen – is it too late to change my mind? About tonight? You see – when you called this morning – *(Lying excuses:)* I thought I had this date – But I just heard from them that –

CHARLEY. *Of course* it isn't too late!

GEORGE. Can I bring anything? I'm at the super-market –

CHARLEY. Oh no – no thank you, Geo! I have loads of food. I always seem to get too much nowadays. I suppose it's because –

GEORGE. *(Not wanting her to get maudlin:)* I'll be over in a little while, then. Have to stop by the house first to change. So long –

CHARLEY. Oh, Geo – this *is* nice! eight o'clock? *Au revoir!*

(**CHARLOTTE** *disappears.*)

GEORGE. What in the world made me do that? I could have spent the evening, snugly at home.

(He smiles – then pictures the scene, bereft.)

A solitary figure sat at a small table, a prisoner for life.

Alone.

Single.

A single man.

(Interval.)

PART TWO

(One Friday night/Saturday morning in Santa Monica, California, November 1962.)

Scene Eight – Charley's

(The **PARAMEDICS** *act like valets again, as in Scene One, and transform* **GEORGE** *from his work clothes into casual army surplus shirt and blue denims – to a Copland-type soundtrack.* **JIM** *watches, in his naval uniform.* **GEORGE** *transfers the pencil sharpener* **KENNY** *bought for him from work clothes to his casuals.)*

(As the music climaxes, and the **PARAMEDICS** *pass a bottle of wine ceremoniously into* **GEORGE***'s hand and the transformation is complete, the* **PARAMEDICS** *leave the stage.* **GEORGE** *turns to* **JIM***:)*

GEORGE. Do you think I'm still making too much effort to dress young, Jim?

*(***JIM*** leaves the stage.)*

*(***GEORGE*** is about to press* **CHARLOTTE***'s doorbell but before his finger's there,* **CHARLOTTE** *rips open her front door and envelops* **GEORGE** *in a needy hug.)*

CHARLEY. Geo!

GEORGE. Eight o'clock – on the dot!

(She's a survivor, hair untidy. She releases him.)

CHARLEY. Come along in with you.

(She wears an embroidered peasant blouse in bold colours, a gipsy-ish Mexican skirt – all emphasising her lack of shape. He follows her in, admiring her clothes.)

GEORGE. I see you've adopted our native costume, Charley.

   (She laughs.)

CHARLEY. Why, thank you! *(Her nose wrinkles:)* I've just realised that there's the most ghastly smell of cooking in here!

GEORGE. *(Polite.)* It's a delicious smell!

   (His nostrils betray him.)

CHARLEY. I'm trying a new kind of stew. I got the idea from a marvellous travel-book I've been loaned by Myrna – about Borneo. Only the author is slightly vague, so I've had to improvise a bit. I mean, he doesn't come right out and say so, but I have a suspicion that you're *supposed* to make it with human flesh!

GEORGE. And have you?

CHARLEY. *(Missing his irony.)* Actually, I've used the leftovers from a joint... have I told you, Geo, I've already made *two* New Year's resolutions – only they're effective immediately.

GEORGE. Go on.

CHARLEY. The first is, I'm going to admit that I loathe bourbon –

   (– Pronounced like the French dynasty. **GEORGE** *goes to correct her pronunciation, then she does so herself.)*

Or do I mean bourbon? *(– Pronounced burb'n, the American way.)* I always pretended I liked it, ever since I came to this country – all because Buddy drank it. But let's face it, who do I think I'm kidding *now*?

   (She smiles at **GEORGE** *– he smiles sympathetically but anxiously back.)*

– don't worry! This is *not* a prelude to an attack of the Buddy-blues! *(Quickly.)* My other resolution is that I'm going to stop *denying* that that infuriating accusation is true –

GEORGE. Which accusation?

CHARLEY. Women *do* mix their drinks too strong! I suppose it's part of our terrible anxiety to please... so let's begin the new regime as of now, shall we? You mix your own drink – and mine too – and I'd like a vodka and tonic, please.

> *(She's obviously had a couple of woman-mixed V&Ts already. Her hands fumble as she lights a cigarette – Indonesian ashtray overflowing with lipstick-marked stubs.)*

It was sweet of you to come tonight, Geo.

> *(He grins as he makes his way over to the kitchen, says nothing.)*

You broke your other appointment, didn't you?

GEORGE. I did not! I told you on the phone – these people cancelled, at the last minute –

> *(He mixes the drinks. Her V&T is more T than V; his scotch is all scotch, no soda.)*

CHARLEY. Oh, Geo dear, come off it! You know, I sometimes think that whenever you do something really sweet, you're ashamed of it afterwards! You knew jolly well how badly I needed you tonight, so you broke that appointment. I could tell you were fibbing, the minute you opened your mouth! You and I can't pull the wool over each other's eyes – *I* found that out, long ago. Haven't *you*, after all these years?

GEORGE. *(Smiles.)* I certainly should have.

*(**CHARLOTTE** suddenly appears and peeks into the oven:)*

CHARLEY. *(With unearned confidence)* Twenty more minutes. *(Flat, underplayed, Fred-crisis tone:)* Fred called me; late last night.

GEORGE. *(Sufficiently surprised.)* Oh? And where is the fruit of your loins now?

CHARLEY. Palo Alto.

(She sits dramatically.)

Might as well be Siberia.

GEORGE. Palo Alto – where he was before?

CHARLEY. *(Nods.)* It's where that girl lives… I *must* learn not to say 'that girl'. She's got a perfectly good name: Loretta Marcus… anyhow, it's none of my business who Fred's with or what she does with Fred. *Her* mother doesn't seem to care. He's nineteen, for heaven's sake… We had a long talk. This time, he really was quite sweet and reasonable. At least, I could feel how hard he was trying to be… he has made up his mind, really and truly. *(Voice trembling ominously:)* He may be my son but he wants a complete break from me.

GEORGE. *(Without conviction.)* Nineteen. He's awfully young still.

CHARLEY. He's awfully old for his age. But I can't treat him like a child – I mean, I could use the law to make him come back. But then, he'd *never* forgive me –

GEORGE. He's changed his mind before this.

CHARLEY. Oh, I know. And I know you think he hasn't behaved well towards me, Geo. I mean, it's natural for you to take my side. And then, you've never had any children of your own… You don't mind me saying that, Geo dear? Oh, I'm sorry –

GEORGE. Don't be silly, Charley –

CHARLEY. Even if you had had children, it wouldn't really be the same. The Mother and Son thing – I mean, especially when I've had to bring him up without a father – that's really hell. I mean, you try and you try – but everything you do or say seems to turn out wrong. I smother him –

> (**GEORGE** *half protests –.*)

– he said that to me once. And now I honestly think that I do – he must live his own life – away from me – I simply mustn't see him for a long while – I'm sorry, Geo – I didn't mean to do this – I'm so – sorry –

> (**GEORGE** *moves closer to her, puts an arm around her, squeezes her gently, without speaking while she sobs. With his free hand, he sips his scotch.*)

> (*She sniffs a couple of times.*)

Sorry. I keep wondering just when it all began to go so wrong –

GEORGE. Oh, Charley, for heaven's sake, what good does that do?

CHARLEY. Of course, if Buddy and I had stayed together –

GEORGE. No one can say that was your fault.

CHARLEY. It's always *both* people's.

GEORGE. Do you still hear from Buddy?

CHARLEY. Oh yes, every so often. They're still in Scranton, Pennsylvania. He's out of a job. And Debbie just had another baby – that's their third – another daughter. I can't think how they manage. I keep trying to stop him sending money, even though it's for Fred. But he's so obstinate, when he thinks something's his duty. Well, from now on, I suppose he and Fred will have to work that out between them. I'm out of the picture altogether –

> *(A bleak little pause.* **GEORGE** *gives her an encouraging pat on the shoulder.)*

GEORGE. How about a couple more quick drinks before that stew?

CHARLEY. *(Laughing.)* I think that's a positively brilliant idea!

> *(He takes her glass – she strokes his hand, returns to pathos:)*

You're so good to me, Geo.

> *(He pretends not to notice her welling tears and walks to the kitchen.)*

GEORGE. *(To himself.)* If I'd been the one the truck hit, Jim would be right here, this very evening, walking through this doorway, carrying these two glasses. Things are as simple as that.

***

> *(Cut to: Two Hours later. Glasses drained, two empty bottles of wine, plates and stew pot scraped clean. They're now drinking coffee.)*

CHARLEY. I suppose, in a day or two, I must get around to cleaning out Fred's room.

> *(A pause.)*

I mean, until I've done that, I won't feel that everything's really over. You know what I mean?

GEORGE. Yes, I think so.

CHARLEY. I'll send Fred anything he needs, of course. The rest I can store away. There's heaps of space in the cellar.

GEORGE. Are you planning to rent out his room?

CHARLEY. Oh no, I couldn't possibly do that... Well, not to a stranger, anyhow. He'd have to be part of the family – oh dear, I *must* stop using that expression – force of habit... still, *you* understand, Geo. It would have to be someone I knew well –

GEORGE. I can see that.

CHARLEY. You know, you and I – it's funny – we're really in the same boat, now. Our houses are kind of too big for us, and yet they're too small.

GEORGE. Depending on which way you look at it.

CHARLEY. Yes... Geo darling – if I ask you something – it's not that I'm trying to pry, or anything –

GEORGE. Go ahead.

CHARLEY. Now that – well, now that some time has gone by – do you still feel that you want to live alone?

GEORGE. I never wanted to live alone, Charley.

CHARLEY. Oh, I *know*! Forgive me. I never meant that – Of course, I know how you must feel about that house of yours... You've never thought of moving, have you?

GEORGE. No – not seriously.

CHARLEY. *(Wistful.)* No – I suppose you wouldn't. I suppose – as long as you stay there – you feel closer to Jim. Is that it?

GEORGE. Maybe that's it.

(**CHARLOTTE** *gives his hand a long squeeze of deep understanding.*)

CHARLEY. *(Brightly.)* Would you like to get us some more drinks, Geo?

GEORGE. The dishes first.

CHARLEY. Oh, let's leave them, please! I'll wash them in the morning. It'll give me something to do –

GEORGE. No arguments, Charley! If you won't help me, I'll do them alone.

***

>*(Cut to: Half an hour later. Dishes and table cleared.* **GEORGE** *and* **CHARLOTTE** *both nurse another drink.)*

CHARLEY. How can you pretend you don't love England and you miss it and you wish you were back there – you *know* you do!

GEORGE. I'm not pretending anything, Charley! You keep ignoring the fact I *have* been back, several times... I'm absolutely willing to admit I like it better every time I do go. In fact, right now, I think it's probably the most extraordinary country in the world – because it's such a marvellous mix-up. Everything's changed, and yet nothing has... Last year, when Jim and I were over there, you remember –

>*(She nods.)*

We made a trip to the Cotswolds?

>*(There may be the subtlest of soundscapes to underscore this recollection:)*

Well, one morning, we were on this little branch-line train, and we stopped at a village which was right out of a Tennyson poem – sleepy meadows all around, and lazy cows and moaning doves. And there, on the platform, were two porters, dressed in the same way porters have dressed since the nineteenth century. Only they were from Trinidad. And the ticket-collector was Chinese. I nearly died of joy! I mean, it was the one touch that had been lacking, all these years. It finally made the whole place perfect –

CHARLEY. And then you went up north, didn't you, to look at the house you were born in?

GEORGE. Oh, Charley – I've told you dozens of times!

CHARLEY. Tell me again – *please*, Geo!

(He takes a deep breath.)

GEORGE. It was built in 1649 – the year they beheaded Charles the First –

CHARLEY. *1649!* Just *think* of it!

GEORGE. Of course, it's had a lot of alterations. The people who live there now – he's a television producer in Manchester – they've practically rebuilt it from the inside. Put in a new staircase and an extra bathroom and modernised the kitchen –

CHARLEY. There ought to be a law against ruining beautiful old houses. This craze for bringing things bang up to date – I suppose they've caught it from this bloody country.

GEORGE. The place was all but uninhabitable, the way it was! It's built of that local stone which seems to suck up every drop of moisture in the air. Even in summer, the walls used to be clammy. The cellar actually smelt like a tomb. Mould was always forming on the books, and the wallpaper kept peeling off –

CHARLEY. Whatever you say about it, you always make it sound so romantic. Like Wuthering Heights!

GEORGE. Actually, it's almost suburban, nowadays.

CHARLEY. But didn't you tell me it was on the edge of the moors?

GEORGE. Well, yes – That's what's so odd about it... When you look out from the back – from the room I was born in, as a matter of fact – the view hasn't changed since I was a boy. You still see the open hills, and the stone walls running over them, and a few little white-washed dots of farms. There's a lot of wind up there, on the ridge, and the trees around the farmyard were planted long before I was born – to shelter the house – great big beech trees – they make a sort of seething sound, like waves –

(We hear this sound – as before.)

That's one of the earliest sounds I remember – I sometimes wonder if that's why I have always had this thing about wanting to live near the ocean –

(The light, the sound – **GEORGE***'s conjuring – have all turned the atmosphere quite magical.)*

There's a little pub high up on the moors – it's the last house on the old coaching road over the hills. Jim and I used to go there in the evenings. The bar has one of those low, very heavy-looking ceilings; and there's a big open fireplace –

CHARLEY. *(Softly.)* Oh, I can see it all!

GEORGE. One night we were there, they stayed open extra late – a lock-in, because it was Jim's birthday. We drank far more than we wanted, just because we could. And there was a 'character' – Rex – worked as a farm labourer, but only when he absolutely had to. He told Jim, 'You Yanks are living in a world of fantasy!' – but friendly, you know. Jim fell wildly in love with that pub, wanted to live there, to buy it, and run it together.

CHARLEY. What a marvellous idea! What a shame you couldn't have!

GEORGE. Actually, it wouldn't have been utterly impossible. We made some inquiries. I think we could have persuaded them to sell. And no doubt Jim would have picked up pub-running, the way he did everything else. Of course, there'd have been an awful lot of red tape, permits and stuff... We even said we'd go back, this year, and look into the whole thing some more –

CHARLEY. Do you think – I mean, if Jim – would you really have bought it and settled down?

GEORGE. Oh, who knows? We were always making plans like that. We hardly ever told other people about them. Maybe that was because we knew in our hearts they were crazy. But then, again, we did do some crazy things, didn't we? Well, we'll never know, now... Charlotte, we are both in need of a drink.

***

(Cut to: a drink or more later.)

CHARLEY. I suppose, for a man, it *is* different –

GEORGE. *(Momentarily confused.)* What's different?

CHARLEY. You know, I used to think that about Buddy?

GEORGE. What about Buddy?

CHARLEY. He could have lived anywhere.

GEORGE. Ah.

CHARLEY. He could have travelled hundreds of miles across nowhere, and then suddenly just pitched his tent and called it somewhere, and it *would* have been somewhere, simply because he said so. After all, I mean, isn't that what the pioneers all did in this country, not so long ago? It must have been in Buddy's blood – Debbie would never put up with that sort of thing... I wouldn't have put up with it, either, in the long run. Women are like that – we just got to hang on to our roots. We can be transplanted, yes – but it has to be done by a man, and when he's done it, he has to stay with us and wither – I mean, the new roots wither if they aren't watered – am I making any sense at all?

GEORGE. Yes, Charley. You're trying to tell me you've decided to go back.

CHARLEY. You mean, go back home? To England?

GEORGE. Are you sure it *is* home, still?

CHARLEY. Oh dear – I'm not sure of anything – but – now Fred doesn't need me any more – will you tell, me, Geo, what am I doing here?

GEORGE. You've got a lot of friends.

CHARLEY. Certainly I have. Friends. The Peabodys and the Garfeins, and Jerry and Flora, and I am very fond of Myrna Custer. But none of them *need* me. There isn't anyone who'd make me feel guilty about leaving them… Now. Geo, be absolutely honest – is there anyone, *anyone at all*, I ought to feel guilty about leaving behind?

(He stares at her, refusing to say 'There's me'.)

GEORGE. *(Firmly but kindly.)* Feeling guilty's no reason for staying, *or* going. The point is, do you *want* to go? If you want to go, you should go. Never mind anybody else.

CHARLEY. *(Nods sadly.)* Yes, I suppose you're right. *(Hands clasped:)* I think I shall go back, Geo. I dread it – but I'm beginning to think I really shall –

GEORGE. Why do you dread it?

CHARLEY. There's my sister, Ann, for one thing –

GEORGE. You wouldn't have to live with her, would you?

CHARLEY. I wouldn't have to. But I would.

GEORGE. But, Charley – I've always had the impression that you two loathe each other?

CHARLEY. Not exactly loathe. Anyhow, in a family, that's not really what matters – I mean, it can be beside the point. That's hard to explain to you, Geo, because you never had any family, did you, after you were quite young?

GEORGE. *(Softly.)* I *did* have a family.

CHARLEY. *(Didn't hear.)* No, I wouldn't say loathe. Though, of course, when I first got to know Buddy – when Ann found out that we were sleeping together – she did rather hate me. I mean, she hated my luck. Of course, in those days, Buddy *was* a dreamboat. Any sister might have felt jealous. But what she really minded was that Buddy was a G.I. and that he was going to take me back to live in the States when we were married. Ann simply longed to come over here – so many girls did, after wartime England and the shortages and everything – but she'd have died rather than admit it.

GEORGE. She knows you and Buddy split up?

CHARLEY. Oh yes, I had to tell her at once. Otherwise, I'd have been afraid she'd find out for herself, and that would have been too shaming... I wrote to her about it. She wrote back – such a beastly quietly triumphing letter, saying now she supposed I'd *have* to come back – back to the country I'd deserted, that was what she implied. So of course I answered saying I was blissfully happy here, and that never would I set foot on her dreary little island again. Oh, and then – I never told you any of this, because it embarrassed me – after I wrote *that* letter, I felt terribly guilty, so I started sending her things.

GEORGE. What kind of things?

CHARLEY. You know, from those luxury shops in Beverly Hills, all sorts of cheeses and things in bottles and jars. Living in this so-called land of plenty, I could hardly afford them! She let me go on sending all this stuff – which she ate, I presume – and then *really* torpedoed me: Hadn't we heard in America that the War had been over for quite some time, and that Bundles for Britain were out of date?

GEORGE. Charming creature!

CHARLEY. No, Geo – underneath all that, Ann really does love me. It's just she wants me to see things her way. You know, she's two years older; I've always thought of her being sort of like a road – I mean, she *leads* somewhere. With her, I'll never lose my way… do you know what I'm trying to say?

GEORGE. No.

CHARLEY. Well… there's another thing about going back home – it's the Past; sort of going back to the place where I turned off the road, do you see?

GEORGE. No. I don't see.

CHARLEY. But, Geo – *the Past!* Surely you can't pretend you don't know what I mean by that?

GEORGE. The Past is something that's over.

CHARLEY. Oh really –

GEORGE. No, Charley, I mean it. The Past is over. People make believe that it isn't, and they show you things in museums. But that's not the Past. You won't find the Past in England. Or anywhere else, for that matter.

CHARLEY. How can you be so tiresome!

GEORGE. Why not just go back on a visit? See Ann, if you want to. But don't commit yourself.

CHARLEY. No – if I go back at all, I've got to go back for good.

GEORGE. *Why?*

CHARLEY. I can't stand any more indecision. I've got to burn my boats, this time. I thought I'd done that when I came over here with Buddy. But, this time, I've got to –

GEORGE. Oh, for Christ's sake!

CHARLEY. I know there'll be a lot of things I'll hate. I'll keep catching one cold after another, after living in this climate. And I expect you're right – I *shall* be miserable, living with Ann... I can't help any of that. At least, when I'm there, I shall know *where I am.*

GEORGE. Never in my born days have I heard such utter drooling masochism!

CHARLEY. Do you suppose masochism is our way of being patriotic? Or do I mean that the other way round? ... Shouldn't we have another tiny drink? Drink to the masochism of Old England!

GEORGE. I don't think so, darling. Time for our beds.

CHARLEY. Geo – *you're leaving!*

GEORGE. I must, Charley.

CHARLEY. But when shall I see you?

GEORGE. Very soon. That is, unless you're taking off for England right away.

CHARLEY. Oh, don't tease me! It'd take me ages, just to get ready... Perhaps I never will go, at all. How could I ever face all that packing and the saying goodbye, and the *effort*?

GEORGE. We'll talk more about it, I'm sure. A lot more...

(They rise.)

*(***GEORGE*** suddenly recalls a more profound scene – we don't see it re-enacted but do half hear his memory of it in subjective sound:)*

(As much to **CHARLEY** *as to himself:)* That night, when the long-distance call came though from Ohio, do you remember?

CHARLEY. I remember.

GEORGE. – an uncle of Jim's whom I'd never met – trying to be sympathetic, somehow admitting I had some small honorary right to share in the sacred family grief – but then chilled by my laconic *yes, I see, yes*; my curt *no, thank you*, to the funeral invitation – deciding that this much talked-of room-mate hadn't been such a close friend after all... And then, at least five minutes after I'd put down the phone, the first shock-wave hit, when the meaningless news suddenly meant exactly what it said – blundering, gasping, running in the dark, blindly stumbling, banging at your door –

CHARLEY. I remember!

GEORGE. – crying blubbering howling on your shoulder, in your lap, all over you; and you squeezing me, stroking my hair, telling me...

CHARLEY. What did I tell you?

GEORGE. ... the usual stuff one tells... and later, as I shook myself out of the daze of sleeping-pills you'd given me, I felt only... disgust: *(To **JIM**:)* I betrayed you Jim; I betrayed our life together; I made you into a sob-story for a skirt.

(He chokes back a sob.)

CHARLEY. Was I wearing a skirt? I don't remember.

*(**GEORGE** gathers himself.)*

GEORGE. Well, good night, Charley.

CHARLEY. I should hate to leave you, Geo.

GEORGE. Then don't.

CHARLEY. The way you say that! I don't believe you care if I go or if I stay.

GEORGE. Of course I care!

CHARLEY. Truly?

GEORGE. Truly!

CHARLEY. Geo?

GEORGE. Yes, Charley?

CHARLEY. I don't think Jim would want me to leave you here alone.

GEORGE. Then don't leave me.

CHARLEY. No – I'm dead serious! You remember when we drove up to San Francisco?

GEORGE. Yes.

CHARLEY. Jim couldn't come and just as you were getting into the car, Jim said something to me. Something I've never forgotten. Did I ever tell you?

>   (**GEORGE** *has been told at least six times; always when very drunk. But:*)

GEORGE. I don't believe so.

CHARLEY. He said to me: you two take care of each other.

GEORGE. He did?

CHARLEY. Yes, he did. Those were his exact words. And, Geo, I believe he didn't just mean, take care. He meant something *more* –

GEORGE. What did he mean?

CHARLEY. That was less than two months before he left for Ohio... I believe he said, *take care*, because he *knew* – Do *you* believe that, Geo?

GEORGE. How can we tell what he knew, Charley?

CHARLEY. No, wait – is that pub still for sale?

GEORGE. I expect so... why don't we buy it, Charley? We could get drunk and earn money at the same time. That'd be far more fun than living with Ann!

CHARLEY. No – you're not serious, are you? But don't say you aren't. Let's make plans about it, like you and Jim did. He'd like us to make plans, wouldn't he?

GEORGE. Sure, he would... Good night, Charley, dear.

CHARLEY. Good night, Geo, my love –

> *(She kisses him full on the mouth, needily – he withdraws. He kisses her on the forehead.)*

GEORGE. Sleep tight.

> *(**CHARLEY** wanders away. **GEORGE** swivels groggily and flops to the floor.)*

(To himself:) You're drunk, you stupid old thing. Now, listen: we are going to walk home very slowly, go straight upstairs to bed without even brushing our teeth. Understood?

> *(He stands up and looks down at the ocean.)*

You know, Charley, with the fog on the coast, your nest up here seems marvellously remote from everywhere else in the world.

> *(He chuckles to himself.)*

Now, here we go –

> *(He runs – not home, but towards the ocean and into...)*

Scene Nine – Bar

*(As **GEORGE** enters the bar, to his pleasant surprise he sees **KENNY**.)*

*(**KENNY** sits alone at the bar – like **JIM** at the top of the play, relaxed on a bar stool.)*

*(**KENNY** is writing on the back of an envelope, smiling to himself as he writes.)*

*(The **BARTENDER** watches the TV, which natters on.)*

*(**GEORGE** smiles, approaches **KENNY**.)*

GEORGE. Hello, there, Kenny.

*(**KENNY** turns, laughs loudly.)*

KENNY. Hello, sir.

*(**KENNY** scrumples up the envelope and tosses it into the trash can behind the bar.)*

GEORGE. *(Eyes following the trajectory of the scrunched up envelope.)* What did you do that for?

KENNY. Oh. Nothing.

GEORGE. I disturbed you. You were writing.

KENNY. It was nothing. Only a poem.

GEORGE. And now it's lost to the world!

KENNY. I'll remember it. Now I've written it down.

GEORGE. Would you say it for me?

KENNY. *(In convulsions of laughter.)* It's crazy. It's – *(Gulping down his giggles.)* – It's a – a haiku!

GEORGE. Well, what's so crazy about a haiku?

KENNY. I'd have to count the syllables first.

*(**KENNY** makes no effort to, or indication that he's bothered – so **GEORGE** changes tack.)*

GEORGE. I didn't expect to see you in this neck of the woods. Don't you live on the other side of town, near campus?

KENNY. That's right. Only sometimes I like to get away from there.

GEORGE. But imagine your happening to pick on this particular bar!

KENNY. Oh, that was because one of the kids told me you're in here a lot.

GEORGE. *(A little too eagerly.)* You mean, you came out here to see me?

*(**KENNY** shrugs with a teasing smile.)*

KENNY. I thought I'd see what kind of a joint it was.

GEORGE. It's nothing now. It used to be quite something though.

*(As **GEORGE** describes its glory days, it takes on that character:)*

Even after the War was long over, a sign over the bar said: 'In case of a direct hit, we close immediately.'

*(**KENNY** laughs.)*

Funny, of course – yet out across the bay, there lies a Japanese submarine full of real dead Japanese.

*(And now **GEORGE** tells it as it is – in his memory it almost takes shape all around him, the lights and smoke, jazz trumpet, the noise:)*

You used to push aside a little blackout curtain and elbow your way through a jam-packed bar – space enough to flirt, but you couldn't fight; there wasn't even room to smack someone's face. For that, you had to step outside. Oh, the bloody battles and the sidewalk vomitings! The siren-wailing arrival of the police, the sudden swoopings of the shore patrol. The mad spree, the magic squalor of those hot nights, the whole shore alive with tongues of flame, that glorious Indian summer of lust...

(**GEORGE** *seems lost in the memory.*)

KENNY. Sir? Sir? Lost you there for a moment? You okay?

(*The* **BARTENDER** *continues to stare at the babbling TV.*)

GEORGE. (*To* **KENNY**:) The glory has faded. It's been what they dare call 'redecorated', that's to say 'desecrated' for blank-faced strangers; there's a new jukebox, that television high up on the wall – but I've gotten accustomed to coming here. You see, I live very close.

KENNY. Camphor Tree Lane?

GEORGE. How in the world did you know that?

KENNY. Is it supposed to be a secret?

GEORGE. Why no – of course not! I have students come over to see me, now and then. I mean, about their work –

(**KENNY** *grins.* **GEORGE** *adds, feebly:*)

You seem to know an awful lot about me and my habits. A lot more than I know about any of you –

KENNY. There isn't much to know about us, I guess! (*Giving* **GEORGE** *a teasing challenging look:*) What would you like to know about us, sir?

GEORGE. Oh, I'll think of something. Give me time… Say, what are you drinking?

KENNY. *(Giggles.)* Nothing! *(Of the* **BARTENDER***:)* Hasn't even noticed me yet.

> *(The* **BARTENDER** *continues to be absorbed by the TV.)*

GEORGE. Well, what'll you have?

KENNY. What are you having, sir?

GEORGE. Scotch.

KENNY. Okay.

GEORGE. *(Loudly to the* **BARTENDER***.)* Scotch – no ice – twice.

BARTENDER. *(Eyes not shifting from the TV.)* The kid got ID?

GEORGE. *(Stiffly.)* Do you really think I'd be such an idiot as to try to buy drinks for a minor?

BARTENDER. *(Thick-skinned.)* We have to check.

> *(***KENNY** *proffers his ID. The* **BARTENDER** *checks – fixes the drinks –* **GEORGE** *feels a brief spurt of powerless rage, rather than triumph. Then it's gone.)*

GEORGE. *(To* **KENNY***.)* How did you get here? In your car?

KENNY. I don't have one. Lois drove me.

GEORGE. Where's Lois now, then?

KENNY. Gone home, I guess.

> *(***GEORGE** *senses something's not quite in order.* **KENNY** *adds vaguely:)*

I thought I'd walk around for a while.

GEORGE. But how'll you get back?

KENNY. Oh. I'll manage.

(The drinks arrive.)

GEORGE. Look, why don't we sit over there, at the table in the corner? That damned television keeps catching my eye – sends you into a cow-daze, just staring at it.

KENNY. All right.

(They relocate.)

GEORGE. I've still got my pencil sharpener.

*(**GEORGE** tosses it on the table.)*

KENNY. *(Laughs.)* I already lost mine!

*(**GEORGE** toasts with his scotch:)*

GEORGE. A Platonic Dialogue!

KENNY. Sir?

GEORGE. Between Youth and Age.

*(They beam at each other. They say nothing. **GEORGE** commands **KENNY**:)*

Say something.

KENNY. Do I have to?

GEORGE. Yes.

KENNY. What'll I say!

GEORGE. Anything. Anything that seems to be important, right now.

KENNY. That's the trouble.

GEORGE. What is?

KENNY. I don't know what is important and what isn't. I feel like my head is stopped up with stuff that doesn't matter – I mean, matter to me.

GEORGE. Such as –

KENNY. Look, I don't mean to be personal, sir – but – well, the stuff our classes are about –

GEORGE. That doesn't matter to you?

KENNY. Jesus Christ, sir – I *said* I wasn't being personal! Yours are a whole lot better than most; we all think that. And you do try to make the books fit in with what's going on, nowadays – only, it's not your fault, but – we always seem to end up bogged down in the Past –

GEORGE. The Past?

KENNY. Like this morning, with Tithonus. Look, I don't want to pan the Past; maybe it'll mean a whole lot to me when I'm older. All I'm saying is, the Past doesn't really matter to most kids my age. When we talk like it does, we're just being polite. I guess that's because we don't have any pasts of our own – except stuff we want to forget, like things in high school, and times we acted like idiots –

GEORGE. Well, fine! I can understand that. You don't need the Past, yet. You've got the Present.

KENNY. Oh, but the Present's a real drag! I despise the Present – I mean, the way it is right now – I mean, tonight's an exception, of course –

   (**GEORGE** *laughs.*)

What are you laughing at, sir?

GEORGE. (*Noisy.*) Tonight *sí!* The Present – *no!* Drink to tonight!

   (*He does so, with a flourish.* **KENNY** *likewise.*)

KENNY. Tonight, *sí!*

GEORGE. Okay. The Past – no help! The Present – no good! But there's one thing you can't deny: you're stuck with the Future.

KENNY. I guess we are. What's left of it.

GEORGE. Death.

KENNY. Death?

GEORGE. That's what I said.

KENNY. I don't get you.

GEORGE. I said Death. I said, do you think about Death a lot?

> *(If he hadn't before,* **GEORGE** *has now reached the tipping point of alcohol consumption.)*

KENNY. Why, no. Hardly at all. Why?

GEORGE. The Future – that's where Death is.

KENNY. Oh – yeah. Yeah – maybe you've got a point there.

> *(***KENNY** *grins.)*

You know something? Maybe the other generations before us used to think about Death a lot more than we do. What I mean is, kids must have gotten mad, thinking how they'd be sent out to some corny war and killed, while their folks stayed home and acted patriotic. But it won't be like that, any more. We'd all be in this thing together.

GEORGE. You could still get mad at the older people. Because of all those extra years they've all had.

KENNY. Yes, that's right, I could, couldn't I? Maybe I will. Maybe I'll get mad at you, sir –

GEORGE. Kenneth –

KENNY. Sir?

GEORGE. Just as a matter of the purest sociological interest, why do you persist in calling me sir?

KENNY. *(Grins teasingly.)* I'll stop if you want me to.

GEORGE. I didn't ask you to stop. I asked you why.

KENNY. Don't you like it? None of you do, I guess.

GEORGE. You mean, none of us old folks?

        *(**GEORGE** smiles a no-hard-feelings smile.)*

Well, the usual explanation is that we don't like being reminded –

KENNY. *(Shakes head decisively.)* No.

GEORGE. What do you mean, No?

KENNY. You're not like that.

GEORGE. Is that supposed to be a compliment?

KENNY. Maybe... the point is, I *like* calling you sir.

GEORGE. You do?

KENNY. What's so phoney nowadays is all this familiarity. Pretending there isn't any difference between people – well, like you were saying about minorities, this morning. If you and I are no different, what do we have to give each other? How can we ever be friends?

        *(**GEORGE** is delighted at this.)*

GEORGE. But two young people can be friends, surely?

KENNY. That's something else again. They can, yes, after a fashion. But there's always this thing of competition, getting in the way. All young people are kind of competing with each other, do you know that?

        *(NB **GEORGE** suspects **KENNY** of understanding the innermost meaning of life; of being, in fact, some sort of genius.*

> *(Though you'd never guess that from his term papers.) Then again, maybe* **KENNY** *is just very young for his age, misleadingly charming and silly?)*

GEORGE. Yes, I suppose so – unless they're in love.

KENNY. Maybe they are, even then. Maybe that's what's wrong with –

> *(***KENNY** *breaks off abruptly –* **GEORGE** *looks at him: does he mean Lois? Then* **KENNY** *continues, smiling:)*

This sounds corny as hell, but –

GEORGE. Never mind. Go ahead.

KENNY. I sometimes wish – I mean, when you read those Victorian novels – I'd have hated living in those days, all except for one thing – Oh, hell – I can't say it!

> *(He breaks off again, laughing.)*

GEORGE. Don't be silly!

KENNY. – I'd have liked living when you could call your father sir.

> *(Beat.)*

GEORGE. Is your father alive?

KENNY. Oh, sure.

GEORGE. Why don't you call him sir, then? Some sons do, even nowadays.

KENNY. Not my father. He isn't the type. Besides, he isn't around. He ran out on us, a couple of years ago... Hell!

GEORGE. What's the matter?

KENNY. Whatever made me tell you that? Am I drunk or something?

GEORGE. No more drunk than I am.

KENNY. I must be –

GEORGE. Look – if it bothers you – let's forget you told me.

KENNY. *I* won't forget.

GEORGE. Oh yes, you will. You'll forget if I tell you to forget.

KENNY. Will I?

GEORGE. You bet you will!

KENNY. Well, if you say so – okay.

GEORGE. Okay, *sir*.

KENNY. Okay, sir! *(He suddenly beams:)* Say, you know – when I came over here – I mean, when I thought I might just happen to run into you this evening – there was something I wanted to ask you. I just remembered what it was –

(He downs the rest of his drink in one.)

It's about experience. They keep telling you, when you're older, you'll have experience – and that's supposed to be so great. What would you say about that, sir?

GEORGE. What kind of experience?

KENNY. Well – places you've been to, people you've met. Situations you've been through already, so you know how to handle them when they come up again. All that stuff that's supposed to make you wise, in your later years.

GEORGE. Let me tell you something, Kenny. For other people, I can't speak – but, personally, I haven't gotten wise on anything. Certainly, I've been through this and that; and when it happens again, I say to myself, here it is again. But that doesn't seem to help me. In my opinion, I personally have gotten steadily sillier and sillier and sillier – and that's a fact.

KENNY. No kidding, sir? You can't mean that! You mean, sillier than when you were young?

GEORGE. Much, much sillier.

KENNY. I'll be darned… Then experience is no use at all? You're saying it might just as well not have happened?

GEORGE. No. I'm not saying that. I only mean, you can't *use* it. But if you don't try to – if you just realise it's there and you've got it – then it can be kind of marvellous –

KENNY. *(Abruptly, as if bored.)* Let's go swimming.

GEORGE. All right.

*(**KENNY** throws back his head and laughs wildly.)*

KENNY. Oh – that's terrific!

GEORGE. What's terrific?

KENNY. It was a test. I thought you were bluffing, about being silly.

GEORGE. Well, I'm not bluffing – so what are we waiting for? *You* weren't bluffing, were you?

KENNY. Hell, no!

(They jump up, run out of the bar…)

Scene Ten – Beach

*(... **KENNY** and **GEORGE** run across the highway onto the dark beach.)*

(They both scramble out of their clothes and run into the waves, laughing, gasping.)

*(**GEORGE** flounders in the shallows, then walks back into the sea, open-armed – to be reborn, to receive the baptism of the surf. The wave and breath and birth sounds merge in a cacophony.)*

*(**GEORGE** is overwhelmed by a huge roaring wave – flapping, kicking – and **KENNY** drags him out, hands under his armpits, groggy-legged.)*

KENNY. That's enough for now!

GEORGE. *(Salt-water drunk, gasping.)* I'm all right.

*(**GEORGE** makes to return to the water.)*

KENNY. Well, *I'm* not – I'm cold.

*(He towels **GEORGE**, Nanny-like, with his own shirt (not **GEORGE**'s), until **GEORGE** asks him to stop because his back is sore.)*

GEORGE. Yow!

KENNY. Can we go back to your place, sir?

GEORGE. Sure.

*(**KENNY** picks up his clothes and turns towards the highway and the lights.)*

Are you crazy?

KENNY. *(Looking back, grinning.)* What's the matter?

GEORGE. You're going to walk all the way there, like that? They'd call the cops!

KENNY. *(Shrugs, good-humouredly.)* Nobody will see us. We're invisible!

> *(Nonetheless, they both get dressed.* **KENNY** *puts his arm around* **GEORGE**'s *shoulder:)*

You know something, sir? They oughtn't to let you out on your own, you're liable to get into trouble.

> *(They stumble back leggily to* **GEORGE**'s *home, sobering up by the time they get there.)*

Scene Eleven – Home Again

(As **GEORGE** *lets himself and* **KENNY** *into his house, he becomes self-conscious.)*

GEORGE. *(Curt.)* The bathroom's upstairs. I'll get you some towels –

KENNY. *(Slightly disappointed.)* Aren't you taking a shower too, sir?

GEORGE. I can do that later.

KENNY. I don't want to be a nuisance. Why don't I go now?

GEORGE. Don't be an idiot. You'd get pneumonia.

KENNY. My clothes'll dry on me. I'll be all right.

GEORGE. Nonsense!

*(***KENNY*** goes upstairs, takes a shower.)*

*(***GEORGE*** undresses and puts on a thick white terrycloth bathrobe.)*

(He puts the kettle on, fixes some sandwiches, sets it all out on a tray. Pours himself a Scotch.)

(Once the kettle's boiled, **KENNY** *enters, washed and dried, sporting a wraparound blanket awkwardly, saved-from-shipwreck style.)*

I'm sorry I no longer have any clothes your size. Yours'll be dry soon.

KENNY. You live here all by yourself, sir?

GEORGE. Yes. Does that surprise you?

KENNY. No. One of the kids said he thought you did.

GEORGE. As a matter of fact, I used to share this place with a friend.

>   (**KENNY** *shows no interest about the friend.*)

KENNY. You don't even have a cat or a dog or anything?

GEORGE. *(A bit defensive.)* You think I should?

KENNY. Hell, no! Didn't Baudelaire say they're liable to turn into demons and take over your life?

GEORGE. Something like that... This friend of mine had lots of animals, and they didn't seem to take *us* over... Of course, it's different when there's two of you. We agreed that neither of us would want to keep on the animals if the other wasn't there –

>   (**KENNY** *is absolutely incurious – concentrates on taking a big bite of his sandwich.*)

Is it all right?

>   (**KENNY** *grins at* **GEORGE**, *mouth full. Swallows.*)

KENNY. You know something, sir? I believe you've discovered the secret of the perfect life!

GEORGE. I have?

>   (**GEORGE** *gulps his scotch.*)

KENNY. You don't realise how many kids my age dream about the kind of set-up you've got here. I mean, what more can you want? I mean, you don't have to take orders from anybody. You can do any crazy thing that comes into your head.

GEORGE. And that's your idea of the perfect life?

KENNY. Sure is!

GEORGE. Honestly?

KENNY. What's the matter, sir? Don't you believe me?

GEORGE. What I don't quite understand is, if you're so keen on living alone – how does Lois fit in?

KENNY. Lois? What's she got to do with it?

GEORGE. Now, look, Kenny – I don't mean to be nosey – but, rightly or wrongly, I got the idea that you and she might be, well, considering –

KENNY. Getting married? No. That's out.

GEORGE. Oh –?

KENNY. She says she won't marry a Caucasian. She says she can't take people in this country seriously. She doesn't feel anything we do here *means* anything. She wants to go back to Japan and teach.

GEORGE. She's an American citizen, isn't she?

KENNY. Oh, sure. She's a Nisei. But, just the same, she and her whole family got shipped up to one of those internment camps in the sierras, right after the War began. Her father had to sell his business for peanuts, to some sharks who were grabbing all the Japanese property, and talking big about avenging Pearl Harbor! Lois was only a small kid, but you can't expect anyone to forget a thing like that. She certainly has the right to hate our guts! Not that she does. She always seems to be able to see the funny side of things –

GEORGE. And how do you feel about her?

KENNY. Oh, I like her a lot.

GEORGE. And she likes you?

KENNY. I guess so.

GEORGE. But don't you *want* to marry her?

KENNY. Oh sure. I guess so. But I'm in no rush about marrying anyone. There's a lot of things I want to do, first –

> (**KENNY** *pauses, regarding* **GEORGE** *with his most teasing, penetrating grin:*)

You know what I think, sir?

GEORGE. What do you think?

KENNY. I don't believe you're that much interested, whether I marry Lois or not. I think you want to ask me something different. Only you're not sure how I'd take it –

GEORGE. What do I want to ask you?

> (*It's getting positively flirty, on both sides.* **KENNY**'s *blanket has slipped, making him appear like a classical statue of Youth.*)

KENNY. You want to know if Lois and I – if we make out together.

GEORGE. Well, do you?

KENNY. *(Laughs triumphantly.)* So I was right!

GEORGE. Maybe. Maybe not... do you?

KENNY. We did, once.

GEORGE. Once?

KENNY. It wasn't so long ago. We went to a motel. Down the beach, as a matter of fact, quite near here.

GEORGE. Is that why you drove out here tonight?

KENNY. Yes – partly. I was trying to talk her into going there again.

GEORGE. And that's what the argument was about?

KENNY. Who says we had an argument?

GEORGE. You left her to drive home alone, didn't you?

KENNY. Oh well, that was because... no, you're right – she didn't want to – she hated that motel the first time, and I don't blame her. The desk-clerk. The register; all that stuff they put you through. And of course they know damn well what the score is... it all makes the thing much too important, and corny, like some big sin or something. And the way they look at you!

GEORGE. So now she's called the whole thing off?

KENNY. Hell, no, it's not that bad! It's not that she's against it, in fact she's definitely – ...I guess we can work something out.

GEORGE. You mean maybe you can find a place that isn't so public and embarrassing?

KENNY. That'd be a big help, certainly –

(**KENNY** *grins, yawns, stretches.*)

It's getting late as hell. I have to be going.

GEORGE. Where, may I ask?

KENNY. Back across town.

GEORGE. In what?

KENNY. I can get a bus, can't I?

GEORGE. They won't be running for another two hours, at least.

KENNY. Just the same –

GEORGE. Why don't you stay here? Tomorrow I'll drive you.

KENNY. I don't think I –

GEORGE. If you start wandering around the neighbourhood in the dark, now the bars are shut, the police will stop you and ask you what you're doing. And you aren't exactly sober, if you don't mind me saying so.

KENNY. Honestly, sir, I'll be all right.

GEORGE. Well, I think you're out of your mind. But first – sit down. I've got something I want to tell you.

(**KENNY** *sits down obediently.*)

Now listen to this very carefully. I am about to make a simple statement of fact. Or facts. No comment is required from you. Is that clear?

KENNY. Yes, sir.

GEORGE. There's a woman I know who lives near here; a very close friend of mine. We have supper together at least once a week. Matter of fact, we had supper tonight. So what I've decided is this – and, mind, it has nothing whatsoever to do with you, *necessarily* – from now on, I shall go to her place for supper each week on the same night. *Invariably, on the same night...* is that much clear? No, don't answer, because I'm just coming to the point...

These nights, when I have supper with my friend, *I shall never, under any circumstances,* return here before midnight. Is that clear? No – listen! Upstairs, in my study, there's a couch-bed. I keep it made up with clean sheets, just on the once-in-a-blue-moon chance I'll get an unexpected guest...

No – listen – carefully! If that bed were ever used while I was out, and straightened up afterwards, I'd never be any the wiser.

And if my cleaning-woman were to notice anything, she'd merely put the sheets out to go in the laundry...

All right! I've made a decision and now I've told you about it. I have told you a few facts. You can make a note of them. Or you can forget them. That's all –

(**KENNY** *smiles at* **GEORGE** *faintly, just a little bit embarrassed.*)

And now get me another drink.

KENNY. *(Eager.)* Okay, sir.

(**KENNY** *goes out to the kitchen.*)

GEORGE. And get yourself one, too!

KENNY. *(Happy, turning, grinning.)* Is that an order, sir?

GEORGE. You're damn right it is.

(**KENNY** *goes off.* **GEORGE** *puts on some music.*)

(**GEORGE** *heads off on one again – drunk? Yes. A Virginia Woolf-like stream-of-consciousness reverie, for sure. Means every word? As good as:*)

(Initially to **KENNY**, *off:)* – I mean, what is this life of ours supposed to be *for*? It's all very fine and easy for you young things to come up to me on campus and tell me I'm cagey. Merciful Christ – *cagey!* Don't you know better than that?

What I said about the bed in the study – you utterly refused to understand my motives. Oh God, don't you *see*? That bed – what that bed *means* – that's what experience *is*! I'm not blaming you. It'd be a miracle if you *did* understand. Never mind. Forget it.

Here am I. Here are you – in that damned blanket; why don't you take it right off, for Christ's sake? What made me say that? I suppose you're going to misunderstand that, too? Well, if you do, I don't give a damn. The point is – here am I and here are you – this may never happen again. I mean that literally! And the time is *desperately* short.

All right, let's put the cards on the table. Why are you here in this house at this moment? *Because you want me to tell you something!* That's the true reason you came all the way across town tonight. You may have honestly believed it was to get Lois into bed with you. Mind you, I'm not saying one word against her. But you can't fool an old man; he isn't sentimental about Young Love; he knows just how much it's worth – a great deal, but not everything. No, my dear Kenneth – you came here this evening to see *me*; whether you realised it or not. You came to ask me about something that really *is* important. So why be ashamed and deny it? I know *exactly* what you want. You want me to tell you *what I know* – Oh, Kenneth, Kenneth, believe me – there's nothing I'd rather do! I want *like hell* to tell you. But I can't. Because, don't you see, *what I know is what I am*? And I can't tell you that. I'm like a book you have to read that doesn't know what it's *about* – and don't ask me what do I want you to say it's about – You could know what *I'm* about – you're the only boy I ever met on campus I really believe could know. That's what makes it so tragically futile. And miss the one thing that might really *transform your entire life* –

> *(At some point during this,* **KENNY** *has returned to dress* **GEORGE** *in his pyjamas, and then withdrawn again. Thereafter,* **GEORGE** *becomes a solo performer in a spotlight.)*
>
> *(Now he collapses back onto his bed, as at the start of the play.)*

Scene Twelve – Bed

(Cut to: One hour later.)

*(***GEORGE*** *wakes up.* **KENNY** *has gone.)*

GEORGE. Am In Bed!

*(***GEORGE*** *jerks up – clicks on his bedside lamp.)*

(He staggers out of bed in his pyjamas – sees a note propped against the lamp, which **GEORGE** *reads aloud:)*

"Thought maybe I'd split, after all. If those cops pick me up, I won't tell them where I've been – I promise! That was great, this evening. Let's do it again. Or don't you believe in repeating things? Found clean pyjamas in a drawer. Maybe you usually sleep raw? Didn't want to take a chance, though. Can't have you catching pneumonia, can we? Thanks for everything, Kenneth."

*(***GEORGE*** *lets the note slip to the floor, heads to the bathroom, pisses, returns to bed.)*

(Not resentful, in the dark.) Just as well he didn't stay.

Yes, I *am* crazy. That is my secret; that is my strength. And I'm about to get much crazier. Just watch me! I'm flying to Mexico for Christmas! You dare me? I'll make the reservation first thing in the morning!

(The telephone rings, as at the top of the play. But this time, **GEORGE** *makes no effort to answer it and it eventually rings off.)*

What if Kenny has been scared off? What if he doesn't come back? Let him stay away. I don't need him, or any of these kids –

(**CHARLEY** *enters and anxiously attends* **GEORGE**'s *bedside, as at the top of the play.*)

CHARLEY. *(To* **GEORGE.***)* You're not looking for a son, I know that.

GEORGE. *(To* **CHARLEY.***)* So what if you go back to England? I can do without you if I must –

CHARLEY. *(Soothing:)* Of course you can. Will *you* go back to England?

GEORGE. No. I will stay here.

CHARLEY. Because of Jim?

GEORGE. No. Jim is in the Past, now. He is of no *use* to me any more.

CHARLEY. But you remember him so faithfully.

GEORGE. I make myself remember. I am afraid of forgetting. I will have to forget if I want to go on living. Jim is Death.

CHARLEY. Then why stay here?

GEORGE. This is where I found Jim. I will find another Jim here –

CHARLEY. Why do you believe you will find him?

GEORGE. I only know that I must find him. I believe I will because I must.

CHARLEY. But you're getting old. Won't it soon be too late?

GEORGE. Never use those words to me! I won't listen. I daren't listen. Damn the Future! Let Kenny and the kids have it. *You* can keep the Past. I cling only to Now. It is *Now* that I must find another Jim. Now that I must love. Now that I must live.

(*As at the start of the play:*)

AM … NOW … *I* AM NOW … I AM NOW HERE –

(**GEORGE** *lies inert on the bed. The* **PARAMEDICS** *efficiently join* **CHARLEY** *and surround the bed once more, one of them with a clipboard. The heart-monitor bips.*)

PARAMEDIC. Here we have this body known as George, asleep and snoring quite loud.

PARAMEDIC. The dampness of the ocean affects his sinuses; and anyhow he snores extra loud after drinking.

PARAMEDIC. But is all of George altogether present here? Or is he part of a nighttime consciousness, which contains everyone and everything – Past, Present and Future – and extends beyond the uttermost stars, and drifts into the beyond?

PARAMEDIC. Within this body on the bed, the great pump works on. All over this quietly pulsating vehicle, the skeleton crew make their adjustments.

PARAMEDIC. Red lights flash at the panicky brain-stem! –

PARAMEDIC. – Curtly contradicted by green all-clears from the level-headed cortex.

PARAMEDIC. For now the controls are on automatic.

PARAMEDIC. The cortex is drowsing; the brain-stem registers only the occasional nightmare. –

PARAMEDIC. (*Checking clipboard:*) Everything seems set for a routine run, right from here to morning. The safety-record of this vehicle is outstanding.

PARAMEDIC. Just let's suppose – that in that particular instant, years ago, when George walked into that bar and set eyes for the first time on *Jim* –

(*Ping!* **JIM** *appears, as described, sat at the bar, like* **KENNY***:*)

– not yet demobilised and looking stunning in his navy uniform – Let us suppose in that same instant, deep down in one of the major branches of George's coronary artery, an unimaginable gradual process began – ions of calcium, carried by the bloodstream, begin to be deposited...

PARAMEDIC. Thus, slowly, invisibly, with the utmost discretion and without the slightest hint to those old fussers in the brain, an almost indecently melodramatic situation is contrived with the formation of the plaque –

PARAMEDIC. It *could*, quite plausibly, be about to happen – within the next few minutes.

CHARLEY. No!

PARAMEDIC. Let us suppose that this is the night, and the hour, and the appointed minute.

JIM. *Now* –

PARAMEDIC. Cortex and brain-stem are murdered in the blackout!

PARAMEDIC. Throttled out of its oxygen, the heart clenches and stops.

> *(The heart-monitor flatlines. The **PARAMEDICS** spring into CPR action, trying to revive **GEORGE**. **CHARLEY** and **JIM** step back into the shadows.)*

PARAMEDIC. The lungs go dead, their power-line cut. For a few minutes, maybe, life lingers on in the tissues of some outlying regions of the body.

PARAMEDIC. Then, one by one, the lights go out –

> *(The lights go out, one by one, during the following:)*

PARAMEDIC. And if some part of this non-being we call George has been absent at this moment of terminal shock, away out there adrift on the deep waters of consciousness, then it will return to find itself homeless. It can associate no longer with what lies there, un-snoring, on the bed.

PARAMEDIC. This inert body is now cousin to the garbage container on the back porch.

PARAMEDIC. Both will have to be carted away and disposed of, when morning comes.

> *(They pack up, remove their masks and scrubs, and leave.)*
>
> *(***CHARLEY*** leaves.)*
>
> *(***JIM*** is the last to leave.)*
>
> *(Dawn. Dawn Chorus.)*
>
> *(The bed is empty.)*
>
> *(Blackout.)*

The End

ABOUT THE WRITER

Christopher Isherwood (1904-1986) was among the most celebrated writers of his generation. He left Cambridge without graduating, worked as a tutor and a secretary, briefly studied medicine and then published his first novels, *All the Conspirators* and *The Memorial*. Between 1929 and 1939, he lived mainly abroad, including four years in Berlin, which inspired his novels *Mr. Norris Changes Trains* and *Goodbye to Berlin*, on which the musical *Cabaret* is based. He also wrote four plays and a travel book with the poet W. H. Auden. In 1939, Isherwood moved to America, where he settled in Hollywood, became a Hindu and wrote for the film studios. He took U.S. citizenship in 1946. In America, he wrote five more novels, including *Prater Violet*, *Down There on a Visit* and *A Single Man*, and kept prodigious diaries. He collaborated with his spiritual teacher Swami Prabhavananda on a translation of the Bhagavad Gita and produced another travel book and a biography of the Indian mystic Ramakrishna. In the late 1960s, he turned to autobiography; in *Kathleen and Frank*, *Christopher and His Kind* and *My Guru and His Disciple*, Isherwood openly articulated the gay identity he had only implied in his fiction. Among his last work is *October*, one month of his diary with drawings by his partner from 1953 onward, American painter Don Bachardy.

ABOUT THE ADAPTER

Simon Reade's adaptations include: Michael Morpurgo's *Private Peaceful* (also published by Concord/Samuel French in both solo and ensemble versions), *An Elephant in the Garden*, *Toro! Toro!* and *Twist of Gold*; Jane Austen's *Pride & Prejudice*; Charles Dickens' *David Copperfield*; E.M. Forster's *A Room With A View*; Penelope Lively's *Moon Tiger*; Salman Rushdie's *Midnight's Children*; Ted Hughes' *Tales from Ovid*; Philip Pullman's *The Scarecrow & His Servant*; Geraldine McCaughrean's *Not the End of the World*; and Lewis Carroll's *Alice's Adventures in Wonderland* (TMA Award Best Show for Young People). His screenplays include: *Private Peaceful* (Goldcrest 2012) and *Journey's End* (Lionsgate/BFI 2016).

www.ingramcontent.com/pod-product-compliance
Ingram Content Group UK Ltd.
Pitfield, Milton Keynes, MK11 3LW, UK
UKHW021839210426
5322IPUK00022B/379